I0221731

New Institutes

New Institutes

*A Primer of Practical Theology
for Twenty-First-Century America*

D. C. WEISER

RESOURCE *Publications* · Eugene, Oregon

NEW INSTITUTES
A Primer of Practical Theology for Twenty-First-Century America

Copyright © 2019 D. C. Weiser. All rights reserved. Except for brief quotations in critical publications or reviews, no part of this book may be reproduced in any manner without prior written permission from the publisher. Write: Permissions, Wipf and Stock Publishers, 199 W. 8th Ave., Suite 3, Eugene, OR 97401.

Resource Publications
An Imprint of Wipf and Stock Publishers
199 W. 8th Ave., Suite 3
Eugene, OR 97401

www.wipfandstock.com

PAPERBACK ISBN: 978-1-5326-8144-8
HARDCOVER ISBN: 978-1-5326-8145-5
EBOOK ISBN: 978-1-5326-8146-2

Manufactured in the U.S.A.   04/16/19

For Christian E. Hauer Jr.
mentor, teacher, friend, and a second father to me

As far as language could go, he would say how and why God actually operates. He would not be content with worship and ignorance, and because scientific law and the method of perception were the great discoveries of his age, he applied them to God, and emerged with a description of the indescribable.

—PERRY MILLER, *JONATHAN EDWARDS*

Every moment and every act is of equal importance in the drama of salvation.

—PERRY MILLER, "JOHN BUNYAN'S PILGRIM'S PROGRESS"

Contents

Apologia | 1

Part One: Faith
1 America and Religion | 11
2 No Name God | 16
3 Kingdom of *Thumôs* | 26

Part Two: Death
4 Money Changers in the Temple | 37
5 Divinity | 43
6 Morality and Religion | 50

Part Three: Resurrection
7 Gods and Goddesses | 63
8 One True God | 67
9 America and Morality | 72

Appendix I: Classic Proofs of God's Existence | 77
Appendix II: A Primer of Logic & Epistemology | 82

Bibliography | 91
Index | 97

Apologia

FOR A POET AND novelist, educated broadly in the liberal arts and trained in philosophy, to write a book of transparent practical theology may seem surprising to some. I am no enemy of religiosity or religion though, like many Americans reared in the bosom of Calvinism, I survived my adolescent trial by fire and a brief flirtation with atheism. An account of my background and credentials is therefore in order.

Raised as a Presbyterian in St. Louis, I cut my teeth on works like Paul Tillich's *Dynamics of Faith*, *The Shaking of the Foundations*, *The Courage to Be*, and John Gates's *Christendom Revisited*. When I learned that Gates, a Kierkegaard scholar, taught at Westminster College in Fulton, Missouri, I set out to prepare for a life in the ministry.

Gates retired my freshman year, but continued to keep an office as Professor Emeritus. Nicknamed "Pearly" Gates by the students who loved him, John was about as near to a Protestant "divine" as I am ever likely to meet; he possessed a personal authority that matched his scholarship. I watched him single-handedly divest a young charismatic upstart of his claim to religious authenticity, defusing a potentially ugly situation and schism in the local community; he did it exclusively by the power of luminous speech.

John and I became friends, serving together for several years on Westminster's Religious Life Committee. Toward the end of his life, Gates broke with the church[1] in which he had been nurtured as an ordained minister, a teacher, and an intellectual. The fault line was the Vietnam War; John believed that the Protestant Church in America had become "demonic" by supporting the state in conducting an unjust war. While he broke with the institutional church that fostered his growth and career, Gates's faith remained intact and above reproach.

It took me two years to disengage from my original career plan, during which time I read voraciously in a variety of disciplines, delving deeply into primary sources, without any clear plan as to degree or culmination beyond my inchoate belief that a poet should be well educated. I found another teacher, mentor, and friend in a Vanderbilt polymath named Christian E. Hauer. Under Chris's tutelage, I stretched my intellectual wings, exploring theology and philosophy in works by Tillich, Bonhoeffer, Barth, Husserl's phenomenology, and Paul Ricoeur's *Fallible Man* and *The Symbolism of Evil*. My growing commitment to poetry and literature led me to ponder the role of mysticism in traditional religious life. Chris's seminar on "Contemporary Jewish Thought" deepened my appreciation and understanding of the Judeo-Christian heritage. Together, we collaborated on *The Space Age Mythology*, an upper level seminar that examined and explored the overlapping boundaries of visual and literary art, mythology and religion. Dr. Hauer first introduced me to Paul Ricoeur in Columbia, Missouri in the early 1970s, urging me to pose my "questions" directly to the French philosopher. I was able to renew my acquaintance with Ricoeur on several occasions over the ensuing years, notably at a private dinner the faculty held in Ricoeur's honor when he gave Westminster's John Findley Green Lecture in 1987.

---

1. Both Chris and Liz Hauer have insisted that John never actually severed ties formally with the Presbyterian Church, and I take them at their word. Perhaps "distanced himself" rather than "broke" is more appropriate. This is simply my recollection as a student.

Though I never took Chris's "World Religions" or "Biblical Literature" courses, I did read *The Ramayana* and *Tao Te Ching*, Confucius, Robert Graves's two-volume *Greek Myths* and *The White Goddess*. My love of Greek and Norse mythology, of works like the *Volsung Saga* and *The Story of Grettir the Strong*, had roots stretching back to the gifted program of the St. Louis public schools and a third grade epiphany that I was somehow "called" to be a creative writer.

The teachers, mentors, and models who generously welcomed me to the banquet of conversation would make a long list. But I am indebted to Richard Mattingly and Stephen Thomas for sharing their insights into Hannah Arendt, Peter Caws, Hobbes, and Machiavelli. Besides introducing me to the monumental work of historian Perry Miller, Thomas urged me to "keep writing." I am greatly indebted to Leon Wilkerson, John Randolf, Jay Karr, Bill Bleifuss, Doug Fickess, Roy Leeper, Ernie Mitler, Martine Palo, Jim Swindler, Stanley Baldwin, David Collins, and Wayne Zade for their exemplary embodiment of the life of the mind. I also studied Pauline scripture with Westminster's chaplain and professor of religious studies, William Huntley. Bill Young (who succeeded Huntley as chaplain) guided me through the *Westminster Shorter Catechism* and a fledgling paper comparing and contrasting it with the *Scots Confession* in fulfillment of the Samuel Robins Prize conditions, superbly preparing me to grasp the full import of *The Cambridge Platform of 1648* a few years later.

Like Wendell Plunkett (a fictional character in my novel, *Crash Dummies*), I was nominated for a Rockefeller Fellowship, potentially a year of study—*gratis*—at a seminary of my choice. But, by that time, I had sensed (serendipitously perhaps) a disturbing parallel between the Reverend Hightower in Faulkner's *Light in August* and myself, leading me to conclude forthwith that I was temperamentally unsuited for the life of a clergyman.

Instead, I relegated my religious impulse to the sphere of literary art, to my poetry and fiction.

In 1986 I undertook graduate training in philosophy at The University of Kansas, receiving my Masters degree in 1991. In spite of my own obdurate nature and a neurological impairment (Attention Deficit Disorder, which went undiagnosed until 2001), I did manage to learn. My discipline at the hands of men like Richard De George, Warner Morse, Don Brownstein, Jack Bricke, Mike Young, Richard Cole, Art Skidmore, and Rex Martin provided me with a solid grounding in logic, ethics, epistemology, political philosophy, philosophy of mind, and aesthetics. On the day George H. W. Bush carpet-bombed Baghdad, I defended a 200-page masters thesis, "Hannah Arendt and *De Jure* Authority" (exploring some of the ideas about religion and morality evident in the present work) before professors De George, Morse and Cole. I taught undergraduate philosophy for seven years.

As an undergraduate, I had erroneously believed that science and logic would diminish my creativity, in keeping with Wordsworth's Romantic teaching: "we murder to dissect."[2] I was delighted to find that even my limited mastery of formal logic and diagnosing rhetorical fallacies infused my critical powers and greatly enhanced my creative gifts. My experience as a classroom teacher, though it proved only a hiatus, taught me an invaluable lesson: the danger I had feared was purely illusory.

This, in summary, forms the background and credentials I offer for my slim tract.

Everyone who understands the sentence "All men are mortal" knows that no human being was ever resurrected three days after death and that Jesus was no exception. While there is very little in the Bible that is true in a literal or empirical scientific sense, much of what is there has meaning, and profound meaning at that. There is a better, more mature way to comprehend many if not all of the claims associated with Christianity, from assertions about the identity and existence of God or gods, heaven and hell to more abstruse doctrine concerning sin, grace, salvation, and resurrection. There is no important doctrine associated with Christianity and Jesus' life-mission that cannot be understood from the vantage of the framework explicated here; I would submit further that doing so yields considerable practical benefits.

2. Brett and Jones, *Lyrical Ballads*, "The Tables Turned," 105.

I have chosen to concentrate on three conceptual constellations, each central to Jesus' life-mission and to historic Christianity. Taken together, these three—faith, death, and resurrection—illuminate the whole of Christian thought, which is to say: everything of importance about Christian theology. This is the first practical benefit.

Presentation of these concepts invites our exploring several topics relevant to the situation in which contemporary Americans find themselves with regard to religion. This, in turn, leads us to consider the nature of Jesus' mission, the preeminence of faith, the centrality of death, and the fecundity of the concept of resurrection for morality. Recent attempts to rehabilitate the "argument from design" oblige me to revisit nine classic proofs of God's existence; by examining their substance, we shall be able to determine finally the exact merits of these arguments and their import for religious life. By this investigation, I hope to clarify the proper relationship of disciplinary science and religion.

If the interpretation offered here disappoints those committed to a purely literal interpretation of scripture, I would ask them to consider honestly whether a simplistic reading of scripture that fosters acrimonious faction, enmity, and hatreds—violating what Jesus calls 'the whole of the law' (i.e., his insistence that we "love god with all our heart . . .and our neighbor as ourselves")—is the kind of thing they really want to endorse as religion. As Paul writes in 1 Corinthians 13: 9–13: "When I was a child, I spoke like a child, I thought like a child, I reasoned like a child. When I became I man, I gave up childish things." If it is time for some of us to relinquish the death-grip of childish and indefensible views, hopefully childlike faith and imagination will not be among the things we have to surrender, for these are gifts without which our individual and collective salvation is probably unattainable. "Truly I tell you, unless you change and become like children, you will never enter the kingdom of heaven."[3]

---

3. Matt 18:3.

PART ONE

Faith

> We grant, indeed, that so long as we are pilgrims in the
> world faith is implicit, not only because as yet many
> things are hidden from us, but because, involved in the
> mists of error, we attain not to all.

—John Calvin, *Institutes of the Christian Religion* [471]

MODERNS ARE APT TO misunderstand faith because they confuse
it with a different concept: namely, belief. Faith is not blind credu-
lity and gullibility; it is not even William James's pragmatic wish to
travel hopefully, a confident expectation that things will work out
for the best in the long run. It is certainly not that closed-minded
a priori dogmatism that Charles Peirce termed tenacity: a knee-
jerk bigotry that scoffs at argument and blinks at evidence. Faith
is a living connection among all sentient beings, which transcends
time and space, and a principle of communication that is more like
the Force in *Star Wars* (though without the martial pyrotechnics)
than it is like doctrinaire belief.

Faith is neither a belief nor a measure of belief; one need
have no particular belief or set of beliefs in order to possess or
embody faith, even a very powerful faith. Faith can perhaps best
be understood in modern terms as being very like a social support
network of family, friends, and colleagues, equal in their humanity

and shared mortality, emotions, cognition, and intuitive dispositions—with this proviso: that one need have no actual family, friends, and colleagues, but may be as alone, isolated, and solitary as Socrates on trial or Christ in Gethsemane. Faith is, in the end, a matter of how extensive and inclusive a community one belongs to and represents.

One can only wonder what contemporary partisan factions would make of Calvin's advice to "wait for further illumination in any matter in which they differ from each other (Phil. iii. 15)."[4] Calvin had no truck with those prone to mistake their own emotional fervor for illumination, the kind of enlightenment that may legitimately claim the adjective: divine. For many reasons (among which I would include the rapid pace of technological transformation, dramatic geopolitical change, and the fear and uncertainty these foster for all of earth's inhabitants), conflict has come to play too massive a role in our political life today, obscuring the purpose of consensus as a goal. Consensus is not, as some would have, mere agreement and ideological acquiescence, kowtowing to a party line, but rather something *to be achieved* through a process of opinion-sharing, substantive dialogue, and deliberation; a sifting and judicious weighing of arguments and reasoning, evaluated ultimately by the logician's toolkit, experience, and the power of human understanding. Calvin taught logic and argued persuasively for its importance in theology. His insight here was never needed more desperately than it is today by Americans who desire a substantive religious and political life.

Conflicting opinions signify a need for reflection and forbearance in judgment. Current mores dictate the opposite strategy, yielding baleful results. If adherence to unbending "moral principle" results in intensified partisan rancor, then America requires a deeper and more comprehensive understanding of morality.

I have emphasized the priority of *connection* and *communication* as primitive notions central to our concept of faith. Let me unpack these ideas a bit further.

4. *The Institutes*, 471–72.

A sense of reverence and awe before the mystery of our *kosmos* is primordial and pre-political, as ancient as the first human sensorium confronting all the wonder, terror, and sublimity of a natural world. Pattern recognition—whether of way, logos, atoms falling, fire, Aristotelian being or Platonic form—provided ancient humans with a principle of order underlying appearances, a premonition of how things might work, constituting for them a purposeful system as well as the first model for scientific laws of nature.

Such a universal system we may well term *ethico-religious teleology*. Every religion and system of morality in the world today embodies such a view. Islamic civilization at its height and Medieval Christendom through the time of Augustine and Aquinas retain the ancient heritage at their core. The system has been inherited by Reformation figures like Luther and Calvin. Buddhist, Hindu, and Taoist alike share a similar line of descent.

But our western endowment in religion comes primarily through the sixteenth-century Reformation and the seventeenth-century Puritans who formed the great migration from Europe to the Americas. That tradition, succinctly expressed in documents like *The Cambridge Platform of 1648* and *Westminster Catechism*, contained germinal seeds of individualism and social responsibility; the particular brand of capitalism that emerged from Protestant secularism in the context of the North American frontier in the seventeenth and eighteenth centuries drew primarily on what Perry Miller called the "individual mandate" and which was "exhausted in the twentieth century." By 1957, Miller believed it was high time that America explored the conception of societal or collective responsibility inherent in our sacred political documents. In many ways, our political history during the last third of the twentieth century down to the present moment may be understood as an awkward, sometimes paradoxical cry for just such a mandate, an antidote to three centuries of unbridled individualism, and a preparation for something new and better.

Envisioning a better society and world is no easy undertaking, especially for a republic that fiercely guards its democratic elements. Implementing such a vision is sure to test the faith of citizens. A truly Protestant preparation for salvation will entail self-examination, a coming to terms with ghosts and demons inherited or projected, and the exorcising of delusions and obsessions. Instead of relying on shallow technical "expertise," we will perform far better in the long run by trusting to the democratic impulse embodied in Calvin's maxim for faith: to resolve conflict by waiting for illumination, that is, by deliberate reflection and the sharing of opinions. Even for men and women of good will, conflict will be a permanently recurring fixture of the political and cultural landscape; but from that conflict, consensus is sure to come, as surely as silence after full discussion—if we but wait for it, consciously attentive to luminous speech.

1

America and Religion

You shall not make for yourself a graven image, or any
likeness of anything that is in heaven above, or that is in
the earth beneath, or that is in the water under the earth;
you shall not bow down to them or serve them; for I the
LORD your God am a jealous God.

—Exod 20: 4.

AMERICA IS, ONCE AGAIN, at the very crossroads of her cultural
being. While the nation aspires to worship a God who jealously
forbids graven images, it slavishly serves an advertising culture
conditioned by a panoply of sensuous visual idols. The clash between the exclusively auditory commands of a Hebraic God and
the Greek primacy of visual imagery could not be greater. Just as
the photograph of the blue marble of Earth from outer space uni-
fied environmentalism, the pro-Life movement would be unimaginable without visual images of the fetus. Without the assumption
of monotheistic deontological commands, how could George W.
Bush ever have become president? Caught in the mesh of these
two vast machines, America seeks its identity even while it morphs
beyond recognition.

By plunging headlong on a course of rapidly increasing technological change without regard for consequences, America risks

religious apostasy, on the one hand, and betrayal of her sacred constitutive principles of equality and liberty, based on the rights of man, on the other. Faced with mounting evidence of sheer human incapacity, rightwing "Christian" conservatives stridently insist that humans enjoy a boundless free will and condemn victims for their own disenfranchisement, without any sense of having abandoned a religious mission to intercede on behalf of "widows, orphans, and the poor." The contrast between human inability and corporate empowerment is as stunning as that chasm between the resources and clout of most individuals and, say, Exxon Mobil or the Pentagon; yet most Americans seem oblivious to such distinctions. Do they really believe that the economic hegemony of capitalism or multinational corporations will look out for their interests? Do they believe that transnational corporations are an extension of the body of Christ, as Mother Church was once held to be?

Still worse: blithe acceptance of corporate capitalism's economic orthodoxy—What's good for Wall Street or Halliburton is good for the country—shows the extent to which these same Christian conservatives have embraced the very secularism that they so often superficially denounce. What boggles the mind is how a widespread public belief in the good will of multinational and transnational corporations goes hand in hand with abject political disillusionment, or the carte blanche granted to the corporate organization of the private sector with a pathological mistrust of "big government" and its ability to serve the public good. Betrayal of our sacred political principles by a majority of individual citizens represents a perilous abdication of moral and political responsibility, one that poses a dire threat to this Republic.

The history of messianic religions is full of imposters, from Sabbatai Zevi to Jim Jones, charlatans and deluded madmen who claimed a mystical authority for their deeds (and misdeeds). While the modern bias of Americans is to round up all of these scoundrels under the category of "politician," to do so is, I believe, an oversimplification amounting to self-deception.

Authority takes many forms, including artistic, intellectual, moral, and religious. While I accept Hannah Arendt's view that our concept of authority—inherited from the Romans—is originally and even essentially political in nature, I also believe that such distinctions are, by circumstance and context, fluid rather than fixed; and that they may overlap or admit of hazy boundaries. What we in America should seek is a touchstone of authority in our discourse and deliberations that accords with these five dimensions: political, artistic, intellectual, moral, and religious. That is what I have sought to attain in this book.

My approach is non-sectarian and non-denominational. I agree wholeheartedly with the assertion: "The philosopher is not a citizen of any community of ideas."[1] Yet we are, all of us, citizens of some community or other. "We are circumscribed by the questions we ask," my friend Paul Stebbing has written.[2] In spite of the limitations implied by personal history, language, and nationality, we must strive to think of ourselves as actors on a global stage.

This work is not polemical and I carry a brief for no organized religion, institution, ideology, or party. In a radical and fundamental respect, I am like those prophets of old, a voice crying in the wilderness—except that, of course, I am no prophet and claim no special authority for the views, beliefs, and arguments set forth here—or at least none beyond their power to elucidate and persuade rational adults of good will. I am simply a man of letters, philosopher, and poet who has spent a good deal of time thinking about these matters, about the meaning of religiosity, key concepts of theology, Christian eschatology, and Jesus' life.

America is, and shall ever be, a Christian nation. This is not a demographic prediction but asserts something about the origin of our basic institutions. It means fundamentally that America inherited a complex European tradition, largely fashioned out of the aspirations and struggles of the Protestant Reformation, and imported by the earliest settlers to places like Massachusetts and Virginia in the seventeenth century. By asserting that America is a

1. Wittgenstein, *Zettel*, 81e.
2. Stebbing, *A Rat's Art*, 29.

Christian nation, I mean fundamentally that our institutions have been stamped by the narrow sectarian struggles for dominance associated with that heritage and history.

The story of how those narrow interests led to fostering a pluralistic society that welcomed religious diversity, or how the dream of an elitist, authoritarian, ecclesiastical polity intended to force its citizens to aspire to godliness mutated into a democratic, modern, marketing culture in the context of increasing secularization over several centuries, is a story first and best told in the writings of historian and literary critic Perry Miller, starting with his doctoral dissertation, *Orthodoxy in Massachusetts* 1630–1650, his penetrating scholarly study, "The Marrow of Puritan Divinity," and decisively in the two volumes comprising *The New England Mind: The Seventeenth Century* (1939) and *From Colony to Province* (1953). Miller's accomplishment, beyond exploding numerous myths about the Puritans (e.g., that they were a bunch of life-hating demagogues dressed in black, solely focused on ascetic purity), was to provide an objective narrative disclosing the "innermost propulsion of America." The particular stories of Anne Hutchinson and John Cotton, of Roger Williams's expulsion from the Bay Colony, Solomon Stoddard's rejection of the Boston Mathers's theological dictates over church membership and communion, and the witch trials at Groton and Salem underscore Henry James's observation that being an American is "a complex fate." Nowhere is this truer than with respect to America's tortuous embrace of religiosity.

Now, there are only two ways in which a person can legitimately claim to be a Christian: either one accepts some formulation of Church doctrine (basic monotheism in the form of a Judeo-Christian god, Jesus' divinity, the Apostle's Creed or other accepted orthodoxy) or else one takes Jesus' life as exemplary, a model or standard for personal conduct. Either approach is legitimate; presumably, any substantive claim to be a Christian would seek to merge and harmonize the two approaches. But no creed or saintly example entitles us to embrace any old crackpot, overzealous, 700 Club-ProLife-Moral Majority-Jack Van Impe nonsense in the name of scripture, mystery or "principle." So we come to the question of faith. What is it that we *have faith in* when we claim a Christian faith?

In Book One (The Evangelical Basis) of *The Life of the Mind in America: From the Revolution to the Civil War* (1965), Perry Miller observed that profound religious experience, in the sense of direct exposure to the mystical or ineffable, is apt to prove psychologically too powerful for most people, to short-circuit the central nervous system, and even cause dramatic changes in personality. (Miller dramatically chronicles this very point in his 1949 biography, *Jonathan Edwards*.) Anne Hutchinson's story—her claim to be able to directly recognize the elect in her community, John Cotton's repudiation of her take on the covenant of grace, her heresy trial in 1637, banishment and subsequent slaughter by hostile Indians—is representative of how an intellectually and theologically naïve person can mistake her own charisma and vitality for sanctification and grace, and confuse her own fervent convictions with certitude about God's will. Her significance as a symbol of religious activism in America is profound; and her impact on the culture should not be underestimated. We continue to struggle today with the question of Anne's heresy, her character and stature as co-founder (with Roger Williams) of the colony of Rhode Island.

By risking religious apostasy and political heresy, America is likely to either sink into an oblivion of empire or else blunder her way into a future that will make a Hobbesian State of Nature (in which life is "nasty, brutish . . .and short") look like paradise by comparison.

In the interest of restoring some sanity to our public discourse about both religion and politics, I have undertaken this project, a simple tract in pragmatic theology that seeks to explain, in terms any literate person can grasp, what God demands of Americans in the twenty-first century.

2

No Name God

Faith consists in the knowledge of God and Christ (John xvii. 3), not in reverence for the Church.

—John Calvin, *Institutes of the Christian Religion* [471]

The monotheistic god of the three sister religions of Judaism, Christianity, and Islam is notoriously jealous, loving and anonymous. He is a god with no name; for names can be uttered and written, put into physical form, and thereby risk being degraded into an object of misguided worship. The god of Abraham, Jesus, and Muhammad will not permit his being turned into an icon or sensuously apprehensible object of any sort; to do so would be to limit his omnipotence, his boundlessness—for god is a spirit, first and foremost, requiring neither form nor content. Herein lies the first difficulty for America's marketing culture, with its inherent tendency to commodify everything it touches.

Given the fact that monotheism enters history at a very definite time, overthrowing the polytheism of antiquity, whether one ought to believe—literally—in such a god is a very good question, one that Christians, Jews, and Muslims alike would do well to ponder and discuss.

If the change from a polytheistic world to a monotheistic one is unarguable, then Jesus' entry into human history and historical time does indeed present us with a unique development, though not the one ordinarily claimed for it by Christians: namely, that god takes a human form, a matter that seems to me fraught with insurmountable difficulties at best. Rather, with Jesus' birth, life-mission, and death, every individual person from faceless helot and lowly servant girl to wealthy merchant and royal sovereign is granted the same degree of dignity and worth. There is something intensely democratic about the Christian message, something so modern that it deserves careful and scrupulous reconsideration, reflection, and judgment. It is no wonder that the "cult" of Christianity caught on as the empires of the ancient world wore themselves out: the message of Jesus' life appealed across all walks and stations of life, attracting a diverse audience, irrespective of class, ethnicity, and social pedigree.

It is hardly surprising, therefore, that the Gospel message has often been associated and even profoundly identified with modern mass movements seeking human betterment, like nineteenth-century Fourierism and International Socialism, or labor movements of the twentieth century. Wherever people feel themselves to be disenfranchised, to lack political identity, power or equality with other groups, Jesus is apt to be a popular figure. It is not only politicians tainted by scandal but those facing the ignominy of life imprisonment or death row who are prone to become "born again" in Christ. In some of these cases, the conversion may even be authentic rather than the mere result of desperately deluded egotism. After all, Jesus did not come into this world to comfort the rich, powerful, and self-satisfied status quo but, like Buddha, to demonstrate compassion for our human predicament.

So it is astonishing that many conservative Christian evangelicals can claim a literal interpretation of the Christian message, a sort of "strict-constructionist" Christianity, even while they embrace a capitalist and entrepreneurial Gospel of Wealth and Success, which slashes taxes and dismantles social welfare programs benefiting the least powerful and most vulnerable segments of society. Viewing modern America's skewed version of Christianity, it is as if the Israelite worshippers of Ba'al's Golden Calf have won out over Mosaic piety after all. A common attitude of Christian conservatives today—not only in America!—seems to be, first, to blame the poor, the afflicted, and addicted have-nots for their own condition and, second, to abandon their succor to whatever resources charitable giving can muster. By their account, Jesus is not just a fag-hater; he has utterly abandoned widows, orphans, and the poor. If, as these neo-Christians are fond of quoting, "The poor will be always with us," then obviously the best thing is to ignore the miscreants and have-nots in the hope that, like TV programs with consistently low ratings, they will simply disappear.

At risk of contradicting this popular trend, I suggest that such attitudes merely appropriate the labels "Christian," "Christianity," and "Jesus" while having little or no apparent familiarity with the substantive referents of these terms.

Of course, "No Name God" is meant here to contrast with "Brand Name," raising the unholy specter of marketing (which will be addressed in Part Two, Chapter 4. "Money Changers in the Temple"). The *Deus Absconditus* ("Hidden God") indicated by Martin Luther's appellation is a hidden or secret, even a capricious, god; but he is not entirely unrecognizable to humans, despite our human inability to see or know him directly, or to divine his will and plans.

All talk of God's will and plans presumes his existence. What reason do we actually have to admit the existence of such a being? There are seven classic proofs of God's existence; while they are not the only arguments for the existence of a deity, they are the oldest and best known: virtually all arguments are variants of these standard formulations. Since I have included all nine of these arguments in an appendix at the end of this book (*Appendix I: Classic Proofs of God's Existence*), I will not duplicate them here but will refer to them by numbered propositions, distinguishing their premises and conclusions.

Five of these arguments are derived from Thomas Aquinas. The philosopher and mathematician René Descartes himself offered three unique proofs. Let us examine them in detail, *seriatim*, and see what they mean and amount to.

The "Ontological Argument" is credited to Anselm, a medieval philosopher and theologian; it is also the strongest of these "proofs," at least from a logician's viewpoint, for it is a deductive argument. Even a hardened agnostic like Bertrand Russell once had an epiphany in which he exclaimed: "The Ontological Argument is sound!" It is in fact the best-known deductive argument for God's existence and, while widely held to be deductively valid, it is equally widely held to fail to establish God's existence as a factual empirical matter, or *knowable* truth. Why does it fail? To determine this, we must dip into the logician's toolkit of technical definitions. [See *Appendix II: A Primer of Logic & Epistemology*]

Every argument, whether deductive or inductive, consists of propositional assertions or statements that, in principle at least, can be assigned a value of *true* or *false*. As Aristotle observed, not every grammatical sentence meets this test: a prayer or a poem, for example, is nonassertive in this required sense. In any purported argument, one statement stands as *conclusion*; the remaining assertions constitute the set of *premises* on which the conclusion is based. In a valid argument, the *conclusion* is said to follow from the *premises*.

An argument is *deductively valid* if, given the truth of its premises, the conclusion cannot be false. Every deductive argument is tautologous, i.e., it is true by definition. Simple arithmetic operations, for instance, are all deductive. Yet even natural language arguments may exhibit this character. In the following examples, I have enumerated the premises and use the token '\' to indicate the relation 'follows from' of the conclusion.

P-1 A is greater than B.

P-2 B is greater than C.

∴ A is greater than C.

P-1 A bachelor is an unmarried man.

P-2 John is a bachelor.

∴ John is an unmarried man.

In other words, such arguments are analytically true; the conclusion follows necessarily from the definitions (the meanings of words) found in the premises.

A careful scrutiny of the relationship between the set of premises and the conclusion constituting the "Ontological Argument" reveals the problem at once.

The tightly nested premises 1–6 are internally consistent with each other and complete. Once we accept premises 1 and 2 as true, we are on the hook to accept the remaining assertions in premises 3–6; for if God existed only *as an object of thought*, he would no longer be *the greatest conceivable being* of premise 1, just as an imaginary cherry pie is not as great as an eatable pie on the table in front of us.

God's existence, in other words, follows analytically from the definitions of terms embedded in the premises, i.e., purely from the meaning of words.

But that is just the problem with analytic and deductive arguments: they never really get outside their own linguistic framework and context. Try proving the existence of a particular, actual, eatable cherry pie using the form of Anselm's argument and you will see what I mean. Wasn't it God's existence *in reality* that the argument was originally intended to show? What Anselm actually gives us is a proof of the necessity of God's existence as a linguistic object. One may mince terms, parrying and thrusting all one likes in an effort to discern the proper domains and definitional boundaries of *language* and *thinking*, syntax and psychology; yet one does not thereby escape the central issue. Linguistic objects are simply objects of thought. Something external to language and tautologies seems required in order to establish God's existence indubitably and indisputably—something like empirical evidence. We have reached an impasse with Anselm's nonetheless impressive performance.

There is another kind of argument for God's existence and Aquinas offers five examples, the so-called "Five Ways." Each constitutes an inductive empirical argument purported to demonstrate God's necessary existence. But a proviso is in order: it is fairer to say of Aquinas's achievement that his arguments combine empirical and inductive with rational and deductive features in a uniquely appealing fashion. These five arguments have their own names: they are, respectively, the *prime mover, first cause, cosmological, moral,* and *teleological* arguments.

These are arguments whose chief appeal rests largely on some feature or features ostensibly empirical in nature; or so I shall regard them.

Of these, the first three—prime mover, first cause, and cosmological—are essentially variants of a single argument. The prime mover argument, while seeming to focus on living organisms and their developmental cycle, might just as easily be applied to inorganic life, since planets, asteroids and stars move and change, experience "births" and "deaths." The fact that such things are readily available to our sensory verification (premises 2 and 3, respectively, in Aquinas's first two "Ways") adds nothing to the force of the arguments, i.e., to the strength of the connection between each premise set and its purported conclusion. The very terms in which Aquinas has couched his reasoning, prime mover and first cause, derive from Aristotle's writings; both terms are not only archaic but also obsolete, of interest only to historians of science.

The problem with the Prime Mover argument rests with the fourth premise, P-4: "None of these things bring themselves into existence." If we hold this as true, then the conclusion—"A prime mover (identical with God) must exist which began this whole process"—appears to follow necessarily, in which case the argument is deductive. But is P-4 true? Does a fetus or an infant cause itself to be born? Does a pregnant woman cause her child to be born? If one is inclined to say no to either or both of these claims, then how are we to adjudicate the indisputable fact that the unborn child is physiologically a part of the mother? Surely, in a sense easily confirmable by anyone, the pregnant mother does cause her child to be born. Or perhaps it is more accurate and ascertainable for us to say that both mother and unborn infant are engaged in a physical and causal way with the process of labor eventuating in the birth of the child.

In any case, it is difficult to see how any of this might involve a supposed prime mover, "which began this whole process." Besides, doesn't the process that results in the fetus actually begin at an earlier stage, with the father's sperm fertilizing the mother's ovum? Unless we are prepared to assume that Aquinas's alleged prime mover intervenes continuously, again and again, to effect creation, we are forced into an infinite regression of sperm, eggs, and births leading all the way back to Adam and Eve. By comparison, Darwinian evolution—the basis of modern phylogeny—looks a lot more manageable. As prime mover derails on the tracks of modern evolutionary biology, so first cause implodes with modern physics.

Both of these venerable arguments, prime mover and first cause therefore fall apart due to their reliance on antiquated and untenable science. But what of the remaining three arguments?

With the Cosmological Argument, the second premise— "Creation *ex nihilo* (out of nothing) is impossible"—is critical. Without this assertion premises 3 and 4 fall. Since all of modern empirical science assumes that *something exists*, the burden of P-2 lies outside the domain of physical nature and cannot in principle constitute a legitimate object of empirical scientific investigation. Whether creation *ex nihilo* is possible or impossible, humans cannot ascertain: we can hardly assign a value of true or false to either assertion; hence P-2 is not fit to serve as a premise in any argument.

To our creaturely common sense as human beings living on a planet of similar creatures, oxygen, food, and shelter, this result may indeed seem counter-intuitive. Surely, something cannot be made out of nothing! But if one tries tracing first causes back to a definite point of origin, whether that of Biblical Genesis or imputed happenings preceding a Big Bang, we quickly encounter the insurmountable conundrum of trying to describe happenings outside the limits of time and space; that is to say: we confront the limits of our human imagination and understanding. Although metaphysical claims lie beyond the reach of empirical scientific inquiry, a non-temporal, non-spatial realm is the logician's domain inasmuch as logical (like mathematical) truths do not depend on any physical assumptions.

Like the notion of necessary existence, the principle of sufficient reason relies on the supposition familiar to humans that every existing thing is dependent on something greater than, and usually external to, itself. Just as Stephen Daedalus (in James Joyce's *A Portrait of the Artist as a Young Man*) finds himself at the center of a series of concentric rings including Dublin, Ireland, the World, and ultimately The Universe, our actual acquaintance can never plausibly get us past that last outer ring. Whether we call it God or *kosmos*, the ubiquity of our dependency hardly entitles us to extrapolate authoritative pronouncements about ultimate entities like first causes or prime movers, ultimate existents preceding temporal reality. God, in all his forms, explains too much for the purposes of science.

Because Descartes's three arguments for the existence of God draw out strands from Aquinas's first three arguments, I shall have little to say about them here. That leaves Aquinas's fourth and fifth arguments, the so-called "Moral" argument and the Argument from Design (sometimes called the Teleological Argument). About the first of these, it should be pointed out that the label "Moral" has nothing whatever to do with our ordinary modern sense of the word, but connotes rather what is common, local or familiar to our experience. All five of Aquinas's arguments in fact constitute a set of teleological arguments amounting to what is often referred to as the Argument from Design.

The bottom line with such arguments is this: they all assume what they are intended to show. The fallacy is so famous that logicians have a name for it: "Begging the Question." All empirical arguments for God's existence beg the question. While this does not mean that God does not exist, it does mean that we must look elsewhere for a coherent satisfying explanation. What we do find will fail to establish the frontiers of a new branch of empirical science.

That said, I shall defer appraisal of these matters to Chapters 5 ("Divinity") and 6 ("Morality and Religion"), when I examine in detail Antony Flew's 1950 paper, "Theology & Falsification," a potent challenge to all such arguments. There, with a little help from Immanuel Kant and Arthur Schopenhauer, we will be in a position to elaborate, once and for all, the limits of religion's metaphysical claims, to distinguish the claims of religion from those of empirical science, and to clarify the nature of the relationship between religion and science.

In some ways, I find Aquinas's Fourth Way of proving God's existence—the Moral Argument—to be the most interesting. So I will revisit the discussion of Flew's argument and the whole question of design in Chapters 7, 8 and 9, where I present a rehabilitated version of this argument, combining it with Descartes's Second Argument from the *Fifth Meditation*. My goal there will be to arrive at a fruitful reorientation for future religious discourse.

As historian Harry Ausmus makes clear in *The Polite Escape: On the Myth of Secularization* (1982), the God of our time is indeed a God with no name and—I am tempted to add—no address. This circumstance has more to do with human beings than it does with any Deity; for God has many names, of course. Hannah Arendt's remark, "[W]hen we observe that theology, philosophy, metaphysics have reached an end" we mean "not that God has died, something about which we can know as little as about God's existence . . .but that the way God had been thought of for thousands of years is no longer convincing," is pertinent. If Nietzsche's proclamation that "God is Dead" signaled anything for modern theology, it was man's abandonment of God—in death camps and Gulags, in genocide, and in every pitiless selfish distraction that lets us ignore the world, the people in it, and their needs.

Judaism, Christianity, and Islam worship the same monotheistic God. These "sister religions," as William Arthur Young calls them, are strands of a single belief system, one concerned essentially with human ethics and justice.

From Mircea Eliade's work in the history of religion, Karl Jaspers's Kantian interpretation of God as "the Encompassing," and Paul Tillich's basic notion of a God-behind-appearances, an underlying "ground of Being," the traditional understanding of God's priority over human affairs, his entry into history through the person of Jesus Christ, and the essential nature of a deity who is the source of all value is unquestioned. I neither challenge nor oppose this tradition. What I will do is pose the following questions: How are we as human beings in the twenty-first century to understand the claims that religion makes on us as rational beings? While intellectual tools and techniques can no doubt be abused, misused, and put to perverted ends, I do not share Martin Luther's view that "reason is the devil's whore." Whatever Luther meant—it may be no more than I have alluded to in the first clause of the previoius sentence—the anti-intellectual resonance of this contention is more troubling than the consequences attending a healthy respect for sound reasoning and argumentation. As inheritors of a scientific tradition that holds knowledge-acquisition to be an important and valuable human enterprise, how can we parse the transcendent and supernatural claims religion makes?

Ausmus is once more to the point: "the problem of God" is no longer relevant. It is instead "the problem of suffering"—essentially dual problems of evil and free will—that is central to the situation in which we moderns find ourselves ensnared.

3

Kingdom of *Thumôs*

There is one consideration which ought at once to put an end to the debate—viz. that assent itself (as I have already observed, and will afterwards more fully illustrate) is more a matter of the heart than the head, of the affection than the intellect.

—John Calvin, *Institutes of the Christian Religion* [476]

JESUS' CENTRAL TEACHING IS surely that: "The kingdom of heaven is among you" (Luke 19:21). The idea that heaven and hell might be understood as some kind of supernatural real estate is patent nonsense; the notion that they can only be understood in such terms—i.e., literally—is sheer imbecility. There is nothing in Scripture to suggest that Jesus believed that heaven was an actual place, or that he ever bought into such a notion. "My father's house has many mansions" is a remark about diversity and inclusion, not housing construction or architecture. Even Jesus' promise to the good thief on Golgotha ("You will be with me this day in Paradise") admits of more than one interpretation; the most obvious (though usually overlooked) being that, since proximity to the holy is salvation, they were already there.

Not exactly Newton's hypertrophic Physicist, this Deity is an emotional one, jealous and loving. The God of Abraham and Isaac, of Ruth and David, of Jeremiah and Daniel is clearly a being for whom emotional attachment is imperative. This characteristic trait underscores the importance of the life of feeling and the place of aesthetics in human affairs; it also sets the stage for an important new development, one that will only fully emerge in the life and mission of Jesus: namely, the identification of individual consciousness with the unfolding of personality as central to human salvation. Here is a god who will give both face and name to a slave, raising him up out of ignominious darkness into the warm sunlight of human dignity and respect; a god who is indeed the source of all value.

This defining feature is captured by *thumôs* [*thumoeides*], the Greek word for "heart": the same word Plato chooses for that portion of his tripartite soul, "spirit" or "spiritedness" and which F. M. Cornford translates as: the part of the soul that "remembers what is most terrible."

A Protestant anthem for which I have a particular fondness goes: "Our God, our help in ages past, / Our hope for years to come, / Our shelter from the stormy blast / and our eternal home." The lyric, like that of "A Mighty Fortress is Our God," captures well the origins of the impulse toward monotheism, born of antiquity and reared in the violent struggle of medieval adolescence: it is a Hobbesian fear of violation and violent physical death, inflicted harm, and the desire for protective security.

This dovetails with the analysis of death presented in Part Two as impetus and engine in the genesis of religion as a cultural construct. But it also indicates a reason for monotheism having surpassed antiquity's female-dominated polytheism in the first place. The spirituality of the White Goddess, Isis or Sita did not make much of class distinctions; obviously, a fertility goddess has little motivation to offer succor to the poorest and most vulnerable members of society. When beer and social order are the main objectives, an impersonal orthodoxy that releases passions in an orgiastic rite celebrating planting, harvesting, and procreating provides a viable safety valve for unregenerate societal energies.

Hence, the unique contribution to the development of human civilization inherent in a personal god changed forever the range of possibilities for human beings. The arrival of the "Son of Man" marks an apotheosis whereby the world of men, women, and children is transformed through a process of secularization, from antiquity through the Middle Ages to the Renaissance, a European Reformation, and a "new science" that would reshape not only the world's landscape but also human history itself. It has been a stormy process, whose goal has never been the replacement of the divine by man but the realization of a divine kingdom through human nature, a rebirth of the soul and society. The intended upshot of Christ's teaching is the installation of a kingdom of peace and justice to reign over and through the community of people and nations in perpetuity.

What would a Kingdom of *Thumôs*, this Kingdom of the Heart, look like? In a host of parables, Jesus lays out a fairly complete description of this divine kingdom; but its most salient feature is Jesus' insistence in Luke 17:21, that "the kingdom of God is among you." In other words: it is here and now.

> Once Jesus was asked by the Pharisees when the kingdom of God was coming, and he answered, 'The kingdom of God is not coming with things that can be observed; nor will they say, "Look, here it is!" or "There it is!" For, in fact, the kingdom of God is among you.'

Jesus' emphasis on *natality* is likewise significant: we must become like children if we are to gain entry to this kingdom. Was Jesus advocating that we abandon adult responsibility? On the contrary: he was drawing attention to the emotional life and spiritual vitality of newcomers. Children are notoriously in touch with their emotions. While Jesus does not mention the "inner child" familiar to modern psychotherapy, Luke: 21 invariably offers "the kingdom of God is *within you*" (my italics) as a secondary translation. The lesser parables having to do with wise and foolish servants and maidens, good and bad investments of small sums, all share a common theme of the vital importance of *activity*—of *doing something*—thereby underscoring Hannah Arendt's reductive though accurate observation that what Jesus preached was: action. We cannot be passive or static in and about our lives; we must take action.

But Jesus did not come simply to nudge the world toward entrepreneurial commerce, as if his sole purpose were to justify Max Weber's *The Protestant Work Ethic and the Spirit of Capitalism*; and the action he urges us to take is decidedly spiritual: that is to say, psychological and sociological in nature, to adopt our modern terms.

Immanuel Kant famously points out that no morality or ethical theory can legitimately require humans to do what is impossible.[1] But this hardly stipulates what is possible for humans to accomplish. Is war ineradicable? Can cruelty, malice, and the various forms of viciousness be rooted out of the human character? Beyond the conventional "wisdom" that human nature is unchanging, and that wars, poverty, murder, vice, etcetera are all as inescapable as birth, death, and original sin itself, we have the teaching and example of Jesus, a millennium of secularization, William Blake, Wordsworth and Freud's reshaping of our understanding of childhood and child development. More recently, there is Alice Miller's revolutionary work on the roots of societal violence in child abuse. What would it take to create a world in which wars, murders, addiction, abuse and violence are the exception rather than the rule? Is such a goal truly beyond the grasp of social science and human imagination?

In order to more fully address these questions, we shall have to confront our understanding of the theological notions of death and resurrection.

---

1. Kant, *Religion within the limits*, 94.

PART TWO

Death

If Christ died for those only who are able to discern these things with true understanding, our labor in the Church is almost in vain.

—John Calvin, *Institutes of the Christian Religion* [472]

If, as Bertrand Russell once stipulated, logic is the backbone of modern philosophy, then death is surely the central fact about religion. For starters, every religion promises to surmount death, offering adherents some form of salvation, transcendence, and victory over death. This has usually been taken to refer to the event of bodily death, about which there is near-universal consensus that the natural process by which all living organisms degenerate is an evil curse. Even the Greeks, rich in their praise of human achievement in the face of obstacles, had to recognize this inescapable human limitation. Sophocles' view in *Antigone* is representative of antiquity's consensus: " . . .only against Death shall he call for aid in vain; but from baffling maladies he hath devised escapes."

Though it may not comprise the whole of it, our collective human experience of death is thus directly at the core of all religion, the "major" or "world" religions and religiosity, in terms of its historical evolution and emergence as a basic human activity, along with other primary institutions of science, art, politics, gender, and family. Yet neither religiosity nor organized religion is reducible to a set of statements about or an exogenous obsession with death.

I referred earlier to a "near-universal consensus" about the fact of death. Aristotle held that mortality has its place in the natural scheme of things. Among moderns, the writer Leo Tolstoy provides us with a uniquely sobering account in his tale, "The Death of Ivan Ilyich." There, Tolstoy makes a powerful case for a claim that death is a vital part of the natural order of living things, something that we can dispense with only at our peril as humans. To strive for actual immortality is folly, a mark of sheer *hubris*. Immortality is something best left to gods, elves or . . .vampires. Even could we retain eternal youthfulness like Dorian Gray in Oscar Wilde's tale, to live forever would be a cruel curse, entailing a withering loss of the existential framework and structure that makes our mortal life meaningful in the first place. Immortality conceived literally is therefore neither desirable as a goal for humans nor is it something that Jehovah is likely to condone, inasmuch as it appears to permanently disfigure his creation, likely by encroaching on his omnipotence.

How all this comports with an American culture that expends billions each year on cosmetic surgery in an effort to simulate eternal youth is anybody's guess. What I want to suggest is that the kind of "death" mentioned in a theological context of Scripture has nothing whatever to do with the fact of human mortality or the event of physical death. In the context of Christian theology and eschatology, death refers to a kind of spiritual and psychological *death-in-life*, which nevertheless has enormous sociological repercussions; it is what we ordinarily call: sin.

It is notoriously hard for moderns living in an age of scientific "miracles" like aspirin, penicillin, air-conditioning, antidepressants, and space travel to get worked up about hellfire and eternal damnation. If social and behavioral sciences have improved upon so archaic a notion as sin, they have done so at the cost of increasing our lexicon of readily identifiable destructive and self-destructive pathologies, psychoses, and sociopathies. For an age in which electronic media echo and duplicate catastrophes, tragedies, and acts of violence in a hundred million instances each day, the toll on our individual and collective consciousness can be heavy indeed. Even confirmed news junkies complain of burn-out; the scarified rest of us, who have to keep our heads clear for work, simply find ways to ignore the glut and overexposure, and train our attention elsewhere. If the center is not holding in contemporary America, reflected by emblematic incidents of school and workplace violence, it is hard to overlook media overexposure as a root condition, and a likely proximate cause of the low esteem in which the public increasingly holds the media and professional journalists.

Whether one prefers the nomenclature of modern psychotherapy to that of traditional theology, the experience of sin—even if we define it as the sum total of inescapable human suffering—is not easily ignored. Notions like transgression, blemish, contamination, and punishment explored by Paul Ricoeur in *Fallible Man* and *The Symbolism of Evil* retain a powerful attraction and mythic significance even for twenty-first century post-moderns.

The concept of death described in the *New Testament* does not refer to the physical death of the body, i.e., natural mortality, but rather to what Søren Kierkegaard called "the sickness unto death," or more simply: sin. It is principally with this notion of death-in-life that Jesus himself is concerned: the damaged, numb or frozen soul of an individual who is somehow alienated from society (like the prostitute, leper or tax collector); one who, like Cain, Jonah or Ishmael, is "cut off from God."

The truism that human nature is prone to sin in no way refutes the claim that man is essentially good. There is no gene determining a permanent Adamic fall from grace; rather sin is something that attaches to humans *after* the event of birth; hence, our cultural insistence that infants and even young children are innocent. Even though no human is born intrinsically wicked, any and every person is capable of performing wicked deeds. As Hannah Arendt observes: "Most of the evil that is done in the world is not done by people who are either good or evil, but by people who never gave any thought as to whether what they were doing was good or evil." Arendt's formulation may betray her fixation on the particular evil of Nazi Germany, yet who can deny that she has hit—inevitably perhaps—on a universal theme in human affairs? In spite of the great diversity of cultures and natural languages, the frailties and virtues of human beings, i.e., their psychological, emotional, and cognitive dispositions, are more or less uniform and homogeneous the world over.

So: what more can we say about this theological or soul-death, this death-in-life?

For one thing, it is more widespread than is customarily acknowledged. Throughout the Western democracies, particularly in the USA, capitalism and utilitarianism have combined to produce both a brutally callous yet stubbornly Pollyannaish outlook on the world—a self-delusion designed for feeding insatiable national pride with the tripe of sentimentality and simplistic slogans. While the American experiment in constitutional democracy may represent "the last best hope of earth,"[2] there is a tendency to be exquisitely unmindful of the fact that democracy founded on natural human rights is an idea that is little more than 250 years old; and that for 10,000 years of recorded human history on this planet, tyranny punctuated by an occasional "enlightened despot" has been the norm. This is hardly auspicious as concerns the likely future proliferation of substantive democracy.

The blunt fact is that for the same ten millennia, paternalism and violence have ruled in human affairs. Schopenhauer's considered view of human history as a bloody continuous misery is nothing if not fundamentally realistic. To recognize this is not to denigrate either the brief bright burst of Greek democracy or the sustained achievement of Roman civilization, from its days as a Republic through the long period of its Empire. But it is to suggest a sobering and formidable frame for any progressive or utopian speculation about the affairs of men.

If this theological "death" or death-in-life is ubiquitous, then one of the strongest defenses of institutional or organized religions

---

2. Abraham Lincoln, *Annual Message to Congress* 1862, 415.

may be the existence of an equally widespread system of communities resolutely set against this dominant trend of human history and iron grip of the past; communities that, at least potentially, propose or seek to represent an alternative. By identifying itself with a Scripture (and what organized religion does not?), institutional religion aligns its community with a specialized form of literature and aesthetic, a tradition fostering the principles inherent in that literature and experience. These principles of ethical behavior and right conduct, of compassion and justice emanate from a deity who is the source of all positive value, and ideally converge to a single point in a process of self-development, enlightened human growth, and social progress.

The revolution in human consciousness that began with Freud's discovery of the importance of child development, the way having been prepared to a considerable extent by Romantic poets like Blake and Wordsworth (who redefined childhood in the nineteenth century) seems in retrospect a capstone on the edifice erected by the Christian message of Jesus' teachings.

The Swiss psychotherapist and philosopher Alice Miller has similarly refined our understanding of Freud's revolution in a series of works, including *For Your Own Good, Thou Shalt Not Be Aware, The Untouched Key*, and *Banished Knowledge*, the burden of her argument being a painstaking and lucid empirical theory of the roots of societal violence in child abuse. Not most but "[all] people who abuse their children were themselves abused in childhood" (*Banished Knowledge*, 190). Whether this revolution in human consciousness will provide mankind ultimately with "a way out of the trap" of human suffering is for the moment an open question. But it seems highly unlikely that we will be able to continue our present rate of self-destructiveness without permanently jeopardizing the health and safety of the natural world and insuring the extinction of the human species.

Miller's treatment of the systematic "soul-murder" of children provides an intriguing gloss on our theological concept of death as *death-in-life*. If eighteenth-century pediatrician William Buchan's conjecture that "almost one half of the human species perish[ed] in infancy by improper management or neglect"[3] is accurate, then perhaps the history of infanticide holds the key to a more enlightened if grittier explanation of "original sin."

Recent public awareness of the importance of "Emotional I.Q." and the priority of mental and emotional health over traditional cognitive forms of measuring so-called "intelligence" may, in conjunction with these other historical developments, offer a basis for realistic hope. All humans are and feel themselves to be, to whatever degree, members of a larger community to which they are bound by loyalty and other affects including but not limited to: duty, love, friendship, and responsibility. As Aristotle and Plato well knew, only "gods and beasts"—sociopaths and psychotic serial killers—could live outside the *polis* of language, conventional morality, and human society.

Despite fierce conflicts, differences of opinion, and the contagion of free-floating ideological strife, it is this common humanity that may prove decisive for the destiny of *homo sapiens* and our shared planet. A world at peace and devoted to realizing the spiritual development and well-being of every child born into it is hardly something beyond the reach of human ingenuity. Yet, for such a realm of human creativity and artifice to become a sustained reality, the degree and extent of cultural and economic change that will be required is almost unimaginable.

Or is it? In the late middle ages, the printing press, Protestant Reformation, Italian and Northern Renaissance, the rise of "new science," and the development of modern capitalism were largely unforeseen. Every great change in human culture and history, like the appearance of great works of art, transpires unexpectedly and without fanfare, taking masses of ordinary lives by surprise. Perhaps our best hope for salvation and unparalleled flourishing lies with the unpredictability and contingent uncertainty of our nature as acting, thinking, and feeling beings.

---

3. DeMause, *The History of Childhood,* 32.

4

Money Changers in the Temple

> Believers ought not to engage in any work without a firm
> conviction of its propriety . . .
>
> —John Calvin, Institutes of the Christian Religion [581]

I WANT TO FOCUS on one of only two acts of violence attributed
to Jesus in the Gospels; namely, his judgment and expulsion of
the money changers from the temple in Jerusalem. Specifically, I
want to consider the larger meaning of this biblical event, and to
discuss its resonance for post-moderns in the marketing culture of
twenty-first-century America.

Similar versions of this incident occur in the first three Gospels; Luke's account is the most laconic. There is no mention of it
in John. Both Matthew and Mark note Jesus' overturning of the
tables of the money changers, and all who "bought and sold" in
the temple. What is supposed to be "a house of prayer for all the
nations . . .you have turned into a den of robbers." While he is
certainly no proponent of modern capitalism, Jesus was aware
that people had to earn their bread through work, trade or barter.
What primarily offends Jesus is the location of this mercantile activity—not the intrinsic activity but rather the fact that it is being
conducted in a place intended for worship.

Since Charles Dickens first published *Oliver Twist* and *A Christmas Carol*, the world overrun by rampant commercialism has been a familiar complaint. This should not blind us to awareness of the unprecedented degree to which corporate, entrepreneurial, profit-maximization has invaded every sphere of human activity from school to politics, from bedroom to church sanctuary. An entirely superficial business jargon exclusively concerned with "bottom lines" and "revenue streams" has supplanted traditional political and moral public discourse. If America is truly Nature's Nation, then we might fairly expand the temple metaphor to include the entire planet and natural world, in which case Jesus' action seems to strongly imply a sweeping condemnation of the planetary drift toward multinational and transnational corporate conglomerates, mega-mergers, Enrons, and Global Crossings.

The claim to be a Christian nation is further complicated by America's cultural obsession with materialism, compounded by our having become the greatest marketing civilization in history and only intensified by the fact of our hegemony as the latest superpower. Modern capitalism has enjoyed enormous success; the very process of secularization, of which capitalism has been the chief vehicle, has overtaken the whole earth.

Perhaps as much as half of America's population is not yet reconciled to the shift from an industrial culture dominated by steel, oil, and rubber to the milieu of a service sector economy. Recent decades have found the American people torn by political and cultural differences that only seem to grow with time; political hemorrhaging over issues from abortion to school prayer continues unabated. Like Buridan's donkey poised halfway between hay bale and water pail, unable to make up its mind which way to go first, we seem stuck at a point of motivational equilibrium, trapped by partisan hatreds and the weight of our recent past. We feel overwhelmed and lost, uncertain how to change with a rapidly changing world, while painfully cognizant that we ourselves have been largely responsible for those changes.

The peaceful redistribution of the world's material and human resources is the great challenge facing the planet today. How such redistribution can be accomplished without plunging advanced industrial nations of the West into economic depression, or developing nations into implosion and civil war, is a question of the greatest moment.

So it is fair to ask whether capitalism's very success has not created the conditions of its own obsolescence. Under conditions of global economics, corporate business across all industrial sectors is trapped between a Scylla of ever-shrinking market share and a Charybdis of ever-intensifying competition. Without meaningful global regulation of corporate industry, this formula is guaranteed to foster a cultural climate of cynicism and greed likely to produce future Enrons and catastrophic cycles of recession. It no longer seems possible to meaningfully reconcile the conditions constitutive of a global market economy with Jesus' injunction: "Render unto Caesar the things that are Caesar's and to God, the things which are God's." Everything on God's green earth is already Caesar's.

Caesar is no longer a metaphor for mere government but rather for the *de facto* political dominance of corporate juggernauts like Amazon, Google, Facebook, Exxon Mobil, Boeing, and Walmart.

So . . . what is the answer? What is the upshot for human civilization to be? Well, try this on for size: a world in which all persons have sufficient resources to further their individual lifeplans, gain access to education and health care, work and travel; where full employment is guaranteed by the flexibility of a global system that encourages people to opt out of a business career for two to five years at a time in favor of pursuing higher education and personal development; a world where cyclical famine, genocide, and war have become but vaguely horrifying memories, as inconceivable to the young as horse-drawn carriages and mounted cavalry. This hypothetical world reserves for government its traditional role of monitoring public resources like clean air, water, and transportation, its responsibility for managing and safeguarding the allocation of resources for successive generations. By regulating corporate excesses, government restores to the private sector its rightful domain of economic stewardship and entrepreneurial innovation, guaranteeing the integrity of both commercial enterprise and government's own auditing function, in addition to providing for the safety and security of its citizens.

Such a clarification of the role of government would be a boon for advancing the cause of democracy throughout the world; at the same time, the freedom and autonomy of individuals and communities to engage in activities, launch enterprises through ventures, experiments, and consortia could well revolutionize the power of voluntary association to further transform the planet, reaching into specific communities to build, educate, heal, and empower. Bread for the World, Habitat for Humanity, and Doctors Without Borders have given us a glimpse of the human power to begin something new. Hundreds and thousands of online communities hint at the potential for a second Reformation.

Best of all, the transformation in human culture and civilization requires no alteration of basic human nature, which is unlikely to change anyway.

There are those who will say that, lacking the motive force of greed and lust for power, human enterprise is doomed; and we shall all perforce curl up in a fetal position and die. Such persons know less about capitalism and the human capacity for action than an illiterate janitor comprehends about plate tectonics or quantum theory.

The new world suggested here is one in which resources for education are virtually infinite, drug and alcohol addiction affect only a tiny fraction of the population, campaign finance reform is unnecessary, and the greater portion of the GDP is devoted to research—not just in the sciences but every branch of disciplinary knowledge—instead of defensive and offensive weaponry.

But what could possibly secure such a Paradise for us and for posterity? In exchange for the social riches briefly outlined above, we must surrender the profit motive and with it the right and the desire to accumulate and hoard vast resources of wealth and material. Such a prospect will transform the nature of, though not the need for, philanthropy. The entrepreneurial spirit of Henry Ford,

John D. Rockefeller, or Bill Gates will continue to thrive; but the ways in which we measure their accomplishments and contributions must undergo a subtle yet irrevocable change. The world of value, of human aspiration and enterprise, cries out to be put on a different foundation than the one that has served up to this point.

The answer, though not simple, is far from unattainable; but it will require massive ingenuity, persistent good will, fearless honesty, inspired translators, farseeing diplomats, and political skill such as we have not witnessed since the height of ancient Greece and Rome, the Enlightenment, and the great era of legal and literary flourishing which occurred in America just prior to our own Civil War. Such an undertaking will, in fact, also require a concerted and coordinated global effort.

The next logical step for capitalism to take is its own partial abolition. We need to retain the flexibility of currency and capital if only for the sake of convenience. But the world is in desperate need of new institutions, whose foundational principles and motive engines are something quite different from those which have underwritten traditional capitalism and which today are as bloated and out-of-control as Elvis in his last years, as excessive and tyrannical as the multinational conglomerates which are choking the life out of our planet and ransoming our future.

Make no mistake: the path outlined here is no panacea. No golden age will be ushered in, even under the most favorable scenario. Children will still be kidnapped, molested, and murdered; women beaten, raped, and killed; celebrities stalked by obsessed psychos; whole families slaughtered by drunk drivers on the highways of America. People of all ages will still die of leukemia and heart disease; the AIDS Pandemic will reign on, extinguishing millions of lives. Alcoholism and narcotics addiction will take their toll on individuals, families, and whole communities. The human heart will persist in "nursing unacted desires" that lead to gruesome outcomes. Pride and ego and greed, lust for status, control and domination over others will remain part and parcel of our souls. In any case, death—that comes too soon in some cases, and perhaps too late in others—will remain a dependable denizen of our earthly realm.

But by detaching the profit motive from our economic transactions, we have the chance to undercut the exorbitant emphasis that capitalism has placed, only in the last one hundred years, on profit-maximization as a value that in effect trumps all other humane and social goals.

We must throw the money changers out of the temple. We must detach the profit motive from capital and money, that is: from M_1, M_2 and M_3. "For, in fact, the kingdom of God is among you."

5

Divinity

How is he nothing to whom a divine heart has been given?

—John Calvin, Institutes of the Christian Religion [491]

I HAVE QUOTED HARRY Ausmus, who suggests that the problem of God is no longer a tenable, viable one for theology. Why then does belief in a personal God, a spirit, persist? Why do so many Christians seem intransigently committed to belief in the existence of super-beings—particularly since every sane person knows that such beings exist exclusively in the imaginative context of literature, comic books, and movies?

This can be explained partly by superstitious tradition and by the appeal of conventional morality. Just as New Age religionists insist on the supremacy of the Goddess, the idea of a fatherly spirit who loves and cares for us resonates deeply with every human—so deeply in fact that we are unable to recognize the obvious: that it is the ancestral relationship of child to parents that is the source of our reverence.

Antony Flew's "Theology & Falsification" offers a permanent obstacle to all proofs of God's existence that rely on empirical claims, including all recent attempts to recast traditional arguments like those of Aquinas under the heading of "Intelligent Design."

Taking John Wisdom's extraordinary essay, "Other Minds," as his point of departure, Flew develops a parable of two explorers who come upon a clearing of many flowers and weeds in the jungle. One of the explorers insists "some gardener must tend this plot." The other, equally insistent, disagrees: "There is no gardener." They devise a series of tests to settle the matter, involving bloodhounds and electrified fences. At last, the Believer concludes that a gardener exists,

> "invisible, intangible, insensible to electric shocks, a gardener who has no scent and makes no sound, a gardener who comes secretly to look after the garden which he loves."

The Skeptical Explorer raises the obvious question: "Just how does what you call an invisible, intangible, eternally elusive gardener differ from an imaginary gardener or even from no gardener at all?"

If the theist makes an empirical statement, then his statement is bound by logic to this extent: he must accept in principle the possibility of evidence to the contrary. Philosophers call this: counterfactuals.

Logic and the law of double-negation states that a statement P is equivalent to the denial of the denial of P, or:

$$P \equiv \sim \sim P$$

Now, if the theist's utterance is an assertion, it will on Flew's explanation of things "necessarily be equivalent to a denial of the negation of that assertion" (denial = negation). If, in other words, the theist believes that "God exists," he should be able to say what he (the theist) would count against, or as incompatible with, the truth of his assertion.

If there is nothing that a putative assertion denies, then there is nothing that it asserts either; so it is not really an assertion.

God does not really love us.	God loves us.
God does not really exist.	God exists.

> Now it often seems to people who are not religious as if there was no conceivable event or series of events the occurrence of which would be admitted by sophisticated religious people to be a sufficient reason for conceding, "There wasn't a God after all" or "God does not really love us."

The only alternative to accepting counterfactuals is, as Flew suggests, a religion without propositions. But that would entail a religion without dogma, doctrine, creeds or canons. Unless there is a way to define the role and use of linguistic utterance in a religious context, we seem to be at an impasse.

There is merit in this suggestion of a "religion without propositions," which Flew attributes to R. M. Hare (for a list of precursors, see Flew's "Theology & Falsification" website in the Bibliography). The medieval distinction between reason and revelation was intended to solve this problem by appealing to things that might be known only by revelation; unfortunately, the whole enterprise bogs down whenever we try to ascertain the precise nature of this "knowledge": simply labeling it "metaphysical" only commits us to a nominalist shell game. Truth or knowledge either rest on grounds of pure reason (If P then Q, P, therefore Q; A bachelor is an unmarried man; If A > B and B > C then A > C) or empirical science (Water suffocates mammals; Oxygen travels by hemoglobin through the blood; If F is a sufficient cause of G, whenever F occurs G must occur too) or upon some combination of the two in a coherent and testable theoretical framework. Developed sciences like physics and molecular biology combine a mathematical-deductive framework with inductive observables that allow for prediction and experimental confirmation or disconfirmation.

All religious experience is ultimately mystical in nature; that is why every conventional faith has a branch or sect that protects mysticism. Judaism has its Hasidim, Islam its Sufis and whirling dervishes, Christianity its Shakers and Bahai, Hinduism its holy shaman. Without an intermittent infusion from such fertile sources, orthodox religious institutions would likely die of stultification, crushed under the weight of rigid dogma and moribund convention.

Mystical experience is by definition ineffable: that means it does not lend itself to linguistic formulation. To put it concretely: authentic mystical experience does not send memos or emails to its recipients. Only *after* experiencing the ineffable can one possibly hope to express its essence in words. Many persons have written eloquently about their exposure to the ineffable and the holy, from Parmenides to Walter Stace, Teresa of Avila to Gershom Scholem. Works like Zohar the Book of Splendor, Hinduism's epic Ramayana, The Q'ur'an, and Bible are filled with illuminating accounts. Here traditional boundaries between philosophy, metaphysics, religion, and art break down; distinctions between literary and poetic imagination and the highly specialized literature of sacred scriptural writings fade and dissolve—in a way, such dissolution may prove a blessing, providing a propitious avenue for recovering our sense of the sacred and sublime.

Our tie to the parent-child relationship and the nuclear family is a special and sacred ground, largely defining our individual growth and future development for good or ill, determining our mental and spiritual balance or emotional illness as we grow into our adult lives. All of our choices are nurtured or starved in this soil, watered with the soft rain of pleasure and approval, or by tears of shame and suffering, frozen under snowy drifts of silence, or scorched by fires of abuse and neglect.

When we are "bound back" to an awareness of the sacred or the slightest echo of prophecy in our daily life and experience, it is to the deepest chord of this primitive ground that we invariably return, whatever the particular circumstances or peculiarities of our origin and biography might happen to be. To assert with Alice Miller the putative empirical truth that "all who abuse their children were themselves abused as children" is a logically different statement than the plainly false one—which it does not imply—namely, that "all who were abused as children abuse their children." All S is P does not imply All P is S (since *the class of persons who abuse their children* is not the same as *the class of persons who were abused as children* and, logically speaking at least, might have no common members. This could only be determined by empirical investigation, as Miller has done, but not by purely logical considerations).

Yet, this explanation, even as far as it goes, is only partial. We shall have to delve a bit further into the concept of divinity in order to arrive at a satisfactory account of the hold that a personal deity has for so many today. By way of attempting such an excavation, let me bracket for our conscious attention something already alluded to at length in this tract: namely, the advent of Jesus' teaching as a new discovery in human consciousness, one that specifically opened the door to further unanticipated possibilities for human dignity and equality.

Specifically, it is the assignment of equal worth and dignity to every individual person, regardless of class or station in life, that valorizes the notion of a personal god acting in history and taking on not just the human form (which even ancient gods and goddesses of pagan polytheism often did) but actually accepting the limitations and vulnerabilities of human nature itself. This is the essential step that legitimizes this kind of a god and, incidentally, explains the course and phenomenal sway of Christian history. This is the face of God, of Yahweh, of Jehovah; this is the face of Love Incarnate, which Christ proclaims as the new order. It is God's Extreme Makeover.

Without it, we are left with Mosaic Law and a tribal God, jealous and wrathful. This is the Old Testament God, the God of The Book of Nahum:

> avenging and wrathful; the Lord takes vengeance on his adversaries and keeps wrath for his enemies. The Lord is slow to anger and of great might, and the Lord will by no means clear the guilty. His way is whirlwind and storm, and the clouds are the dust of his feet. He rebukes the sea and makes it dry; he dries up all the rivers; Bashan and Carmel wither; the bloom of Lebanon fades. The mountains quake before him, the hills melt; the earth is laid waste before him, the world and all that dwell therein. Who can stand before his indignation? Who can endure

the heat of his anger? His wrath is poured out like fire,
and the rocks are broken asunder by him. The Lord is
good, a stronghold in the day of trouble; he knows those
who take refuge in him. But with an overflowing flood
he will make a full end of his adversaries, and will pursue
his enemies into darkness. What do you plot against the
Lord? He will make a full end; he will not take vengeance
twice against his foes.[1]

Clearly, this is not the sort of deity to get too chummy with.
Except for that last part about not taking vengeance twice, he
sounds rather like a modern corporate juggernaut laying waste to
the earth and its picayune little nations. Indeed, one may wonder
whether corporate monoliths and their top executives do not se-
cretly cast themselves in just such a role. It would explain a lot.

Whatever the case might be, the God presented in Nahum is
impersonal, objective and capricious; absolutely inscrutable and
formidably aloof. The tribal God of the nomadic Hebrews is a God
to be reckoned with, yes: but He will do all the reckoning. This
is an Avatar of Vengeance who will make you disappear; but not
one overly concerned about the *Disappeareds,* the Disenfranchised
or Faceless Masses. It is the face of an angry Father as seen by a
trembling, terrified child.

Jesus' teaching therefore marks an evolutionary turning point
in the history and phenomenology of divinity itself.

But what exactly are we to make of this divinity? If the analysis presented here is correct, this turning point explains the prefer-
ence of modern-day Christians, and perhaps even monotheists of
all three sister religions, for this personal deity. But it clarifies nothing about the content of that divinity; indeed, it does more to confuse matters, due to the conflation of human and divine natures,
Pythagorean Trinitarian conceptions, as Martin Scorsese was no
doubt mortified to learn upon the controversial reception of his
The Last Temptation of Christ. Old prejudices die hard, if at all.
How is one to understand the notion of a God-Man, if not by paradoxical analogy with centaurs, satyrs, and the Man-in-the-Moon?

1. Nah 1:2–9.

Metaphors—even the best—have their limits; most make poor explanations.

In his posthumously published *Ethics*, the Lutheran theologian Dietrich Bonhoeffer spends a good deal of energy and argument to make a simple point about the unique place occupied by Christian ethics. From this viewpoint, Bonhoeffer asserts, Christ is *the standard* by which every human action is to be measured. He talks a great deal about being "*in Christ*"; but the upshot of all his argument is the consciousness, on the human side, of ever falling short of the divine standard. As if to say, "Man is *down here*, below the angels (or is it just above?)" but when we are *in Christ*, we don't climb the rungs between man and God, we are given access to a *standard* set for us by Jesus—set, one is tempted to say, *especially for us*. Try as we might, we can never remain in Christ, persisting in that standard, but are forever falling short. The blessing and the payoff for Christians remains in the striving, the willingness to be shown, and the promise that, as often as we fail or fall short, we may be granted access to the standard again and again for as long as we live.

6

Morality and Religion

In our daily reading we fall in with many obscure passages which convict us of ignorance.

—John Calvin, *Institutes of the Christian Religion* [472]

Now at last we can try to clarify the proper relationship of morality and religion; and by doing so to clear the air. For morality has a very definite and important relationship with religion, though it bears little resemblance to what is commonly understood and promulgated in the public arena, particularly through the electronic media.

Our Judeo-Christian tradition, and probably all monotheistic religion, is what philosophers call *deontological*, in other words: all moral precepts and rules for conduct issue directly from divine commands. This defining characteristic of deontology and deontological systems is the root cause of imbroglios about placing copies of the Ten Commandments in courthouses; and it is also the cause of a more fundamental confusion of legalism and morality. The fault is even more astonishing in a nation that, like the United States, insists in its Constitution on a sharp separation between church and state. If we are God's creatures, one might plausibly assume that our laws should be consistent with, if not directly implied by, divine decrees.

But, as we have shown, a proper Christian understanding of the different and separate natures of the human and the divine refutes this. Because man is not divine, he possesses no special access to God's will, which necessarily remains inscrutable to our eyes and our intellects. Televangelists like Pat Robertson, Jack Van Impe, and the late Jerry Falwell, who proclaim such access and spurious "knowledge" of God's inclinations, plans, or purposes, are nothing more than hucksters and fundraising fat-boys. Such churlish imps clutter the religious life with their chatter of promised salvation and fear of damnation: charlatans every one, who are either lying outright or self-deceived, their claims about Biblical inerrancy fatuous nonsense. Man has no such access to God, as we shall see.

All moral thinking has an intimate connection with human freedom, not freedom *from* but freedom *to*. Immanuel Kant could conceive that this freedom of morally right action, viewed from the perspective of intelligence or *noeisis*, might coincide with an identical event seen from the scientific standpoint of causal determinism, in which all natural events are governed by laws of physics. In other words, morally free acts are, at the same time, compatible with determinism. This implies no dualism; the distinction between a *phenomenal* sphere of scientific causation and a *noumenal* sphere of intellectual freedom is an exercise of imaginative thought, made for the purpose of explanation. For Kant, all free will comes down to this: acting in accord with the Moral Law. Kant was a Christian Pietist and therefore a deontologist; but he did not confuse divine commands with human morality and ethics.

Kant's distinction between conventional and critical morality marks a crucial distinction; for our purposes, it is a watershed, establishing the boundaries of subjective and objective morality. All of us live in a world of conventional morality, governed by traditional belief, mores, and customs. But conventional morality is neither autonomous nor supreme. It is only by applying first-order moral principles (Do No Harm, Utitlity, Kant's Categorical Imperative, The Golden Rule) to maxims and rules of behavior, directly to actions themselves or to accurate descriptions of actions, allowing us to sift through the welter of motives, intentions, and consequences confronting us, that we are able to arrive at something like an objective framework for understanding: the province of critical morality.

Subjectively, after all, I may believe that I am morally right to keep the money S. has dropped, to cheat on my taxes provided I don't technically break the law, to take sexual liberties with a slightly drunk, vulnerable secretary at the office Christmas party, or to slug anyone who insults me (similarly, with Hitler invading Poland, or Bush 41 and 43 Iraq). But the only way we can attain an *objective* moral understanding of the character of our actions is by testing them against the standard of reliable, first-order, moral principles. And we all know how the panoply of individual needs, psychological "issues," emotions, and behavioral dispositions can cloud one's judgment about such matters. If that secretary at the party, for example, is especially "hot," sexy and attractive to *me*, well, it makes *a difference* . . .but it may not make it morally right for me to accede to my lust. Then again, perhaps she's fat, an "Ugly Betty"—wouldn't I be doing the poor lonely thing a favor then, actually? We can ratchet up the complexity of such scenarios in any direction we like. The most patent rationalization does not necessarily proclaim itself to the internal forum of introspective thought, particularly where self-interest and sensibility are intertwined. But I think anyone can appreciate the propensity for self-delusion and deception where our desires and dispositions are especially concentrated. In one way, this is the beauty of morality and moral reasoning, and of trying to apply moral principles in one's life. It is a challenge! On the other hand, if I have habitually failed to resist such temptations in the past as a matter of disposition, anyone might expect my decision to be a foregone conclusion. But perhaps someone will fling open the coatroom door and shine a light on my dilemma before we get too far.

The point is: without an objective standard, a willingness to sift and weigh evidence, to look carefully at strands of reasoning and arguments, and to recognize how our own fallibility, motives, and intentions may subtly color and inform our judgment about empirical facts, we are really just twisting in the breeze about the character and quality of our moral actions, good and bad. We really don't know. Those who insist dogmatically that morality is cut-and-dry, black and white, that "You know the rule and you follow it!" or "You just do the right thing," must be carrying around some little nineteenth-century pocket primer of right conduct, or else— what is more likely—they are just fooling themselves. The fact that murder is universally known and felt to be wrong hasn't exactly rendered homicide obsolete . . . Those clods that think the moral life is nothing more than rational rule-following lack imagination and appreciation for the intricacies and complexities of human action and relationships. Perhaps they have never really lived among humans with any degree of depth or involvement.

Besides: who among us can say with certainty that there are no two individuals, circumstances, and experience—to revisit our Christmas party scenario—for whom a *different denouement* (namely, one with a more romantic, not to say erotic, outcome) might prove to be the morally right and best one?

An inability (or diffident refusal) to distinguish persons from their actions also flows from this simpleminded deontological position and the confusion of human and divine. Everyone who condemns a person rather than the person's morally wrong action errs by treating what is at most a dispositional property as if it were a sensible attribute of the person, something like eye color or body type, being pigeon-toed or possessing a cleft palate. The ubiquity of so elementary a mistake in moral reasoning hardly justifies the practice. As with all authority resting on tradition, the mere fact that a practice is of long-standing offers no guarantee of its legitimacy. The virulence of conflicting opinions and the barrenness of opposition surrounding abortion vs. choice or the pragmatic merits of the death penalty are infused with this type of shallow thinking, which is no thinking at all.

"Condemn the act, but have compassion for the person" recommends itself as a practical maxim, not least for its clarity and humane elegance. After all: no individual who equates a person with that person's wrong act would willingly apply the same standard to himself. How could he do so without admitting "I am what I do"? However important actions may be, no person is merely the sum total of his deeds; it is the very distinction between *person* and *deed* that makes it possible in the first place for us to objectively appraise actions in the arena of moral and political judgments. Ultimately, it is the act that is wicked or criminal, not the person himself, for which the person must be held morally and/or legally accountable. We punish people under the law not for having wicked traits, characters, or dispositions but for their wicked deeds. Whoever rejects a reductive description as self-imputation is hypocritical in applying it to others.

If compassion was a good enough law for Jesus and Buddha, it will serve the rest of us well both as precept and practice.

This brings us to the question of moral authenticity, for which there is a test. The Moral Law, if there is such a thing, is humane and humanizing; its Janus-face is neither Weakness and Vengeance nor Forgiveness and Bloodlust, but Compassion and Mercy. Kant held that the Moral Law ruled without content, that the Law itself had no linguistic content: it said nothing, commanded nothing specifically; and yet Kant believed that the Moral Law ruled supreme over human action by virtue of its *form alone*. The form of law, especially human law, provides sufficient strictness and rigidity for the sake of punishment; compassion and mercy themselves constitute justice when applied thoroughly through the stricture of the law. Anything else is chin music.

Man is not put on earth to aspire to become godlike or to encroach in any way on divine prerogative; but that does not suggest that humans are privileged to know or permitted to define that prerogative.

Intelligent Design arguments, regardless of the figures and metaphors they exploit, or the specialized language with which they clothe their assertions, claims, and conclusions, whether that of molecular biology and genetics, Stephen Hawking's cosmo-logical speculations, or metaphysical string theory and quantum dynamics, all founder on the same rock: namely, Flew's argument about counterfactuals. Empirical scientific investigation may discover an unending degree of structure wherever it turns its focused eye throughout the natural world; new techniques and tools may unfold a variety of design-like entities; but it will never thereby legitimately infer or deduce the existence, name or address of an intelligent designer. We will let a nineteenth-century philosopher of extraordinary gifts and insight, Arthur Schopenhauer, tell us why.

Schopenhauer made a vital distinction between sensation (stimuli in skin and nerves) and perception (an act of intellection or understanding). From this distinction, Schopenhauer elicited a rather remarkable insight about visual perception, which is easily reproduced and confirmed by anyone. If you tilt your head while looking at something, the angle of your vision necessarily changes and the object appears to have tilted. Yet no one thinks that, because of this, the object of one's perception has tilted or gone sideways. Now, the question is: exactly how do you know that? You have only the frame of reference of your act of visual perception to go on. Not only does the object appear tilted, but the sensation in your eyes, retina, and skin has also shifted when you tilt your head. If perception were nothing more than sensation (skin and nerve activity), you would not be able to distinguish between the two sets of events. Thus, your perception—and the recognition that it is not an object of the external world but the position of your head that has altered—is an intellectual act, an operation of the understanding.

Schopenhauer's discovery is unfortunately decisive for the proponents of Intelligent Design. The significance of Schopenhauer's demonstration and argument for our faculty of reason, to quote Richard Taylor on precisely that point, is rather far-reaching. It indicates, for example, the sense in which the objective world, which we naively suppose is merely "given" to sensation, is in fact a creation of the understanding. No such world, Schopenhauer notes, just "walks into our brain" through the senses.[1]

Although Schopenhauer blamed Kant for subsequent misinterpretations (particularly appropriations of Kant's *"ideas of reason"* by G. W. F. Hegel, whom he calls "the notorious charlatan" and "an impudent scribbler of nonsense"), Schopenhauer realized that what Kant had achieved in *The Critique of Pure Reason* was nothing less than the inability of the faculty of reason to furnish out of its own materials or *a priori* forms access to "a supersensuous realm," and consequently "the impossibility of every such proof and with it that of all speculative theology"! If no human "faculty of the supersensuous" exists, then no metaphysical truths could possibly be ascertained or asserted. There is, in other words, no "oracular ability within us designed directly for *metaphysics*."[2]

> When, therefore, we are told that we possess a faculty for immediate material (i.e., furnishing the substance and not merely the form) supersensuous (i.e., transcending all possibility of experience) knowledge, a faculty expressly intended for metaphysical insight and dwelling within us for that purpose, and that our *faculty of reason* consists in this, then I must be so impolite as to call this a downright lie. For the least but honest self-examination must convince anyone that absolutely no such faculty exists within us.[3]

Whatever Mormons may teach, humankind has no access to the mind or whim of God or to that of any deity. The one true God is wholly inscrutable. We can never entirely assure ourselves that He loves us. This is intimately connected with our nature as human beings. We can hardly shed our nature like a snake sloughing off its skin—or rather, if (and when) we do, it grows back again, the

1. Schopenhauer, *Sufficient Reason*, xvi.
2. Schopenhauer, *Sufficient Reason*, 166.
3. Schopenhauer, 169–70.

same as it ever was. This does not mean that we are insects, God's automatons or slaves. Atonement is our surrender to the limitations imposed by a universe of which we are a part and to which we belong; our recognition of sacred supremacy; and our celebration of God's creation and glory which survives and flourishes in every facet of meaning for human life and endeavor, waiting for us to discover, as a yardstick and standard of shining principle. There is no area of human experience or aspiration, from aesthetics to politics, science to theology that is exempt from the reach of this sublime meaning, which is the stamp of common human frailty and our shared mortality. Nowhere is that stamp of identity more recognizable than with respect to human morality.

PART THREE

Resurrection

If we are partakers in his resurrection, we are raised up by means of it to newness of life which conforms us to the righteousness of God.

—John Calvin, *Institutes of the Christian Religion* [515]

But, if Jesus' resurrection did not overcome the physical event of human bodily death, what sense can be given to the notion that Jesus died for mankind's collective sins, or restored man's link to paradise lost by Adam's fall? How are we to understand the doctrine of a "resurrection of the body" central to Christian theology?

Could all human beings share a proper understanding of our nature as imperfect (that is, not-godlike) beings prone to error, confusion, and failing, turning their religious attention from some speculative future life to this one, then we might arguably establish the prerequisites for improving the world's condition, preparing the ground for substantively transforming the human artifice of nations and societies. Secularization is not merely compatible with Christian eschatology, it holds the very possibility and promise, as Dietrich Bonhoeffer surmised, of "a fulfillment of the Christian Gospel." Bodily resurrection refers to an event or process that we may fully expect to take place in *this* world.

Resurrection and the body: To attain a proper understanding of this central concept of Christianity, we must consider the clues Jesus himself gives us in the context of the original explosion of that teaching in the development of Western consciousness; that is, his emphasis on children and the crucial salience of being *like a child*. What is Jesus getting at here? Children are defenseless, weak, and vulnerable. Is Christ recommending these qualities as political virtues? If that were so, Jesus might have been nothing more than a poor psychotic, understandably put out of his misery by Roman crucifixion.

But that is not at all what Jesus was suggesting. Aristotle knew that human beings are like plants that need a nurturing environment of rich soil, nutrients, oxygen, and water; not like jewels that need polishing. Newborns are marvelously in touch with their physical bodies, for all that they lack in the way of developed linguistic skills and potty training. Whether one conceives it as Norman O. Brown's "polymorphous perversity" or as a state of natural grace and innocence, the field of child development has repeatedly and increasingly underscored the critical importance of the various stages of growth from infancy through adolescence, particularly with respect to an individual's adaptability, maturation, and resilience as an adult. At Alice Miller's *The Natural Child Project* website, the distinguished social theorist writes:

> It is time to relinquish destructive models and to mistrust the principle of obedience. We have no need of obedient children brainwashed by their upbringing to be the ideal victims for the empty verbiage and the blandishments of terrorists and lunatic ideologists and ready to fall in with their commands, even to the extent of killing others. We need children with open eyes and ears, children prepared to protest against injustice, stupidity and ignorance with arguments and constructive action. Jesus was able to do this when he was twelve years old and the scene in the temple demonstrates eloquently that he could refuse the obedience asked of him by his parents without hurting their feelings.

> With the best will in the world we cannot truly emu-
> late the example of Jesus. To do that we would need to
> have been through an entirely different kind of personal
> history.

By reclaiming our bodies and childhood selves, we reclaim
and recover our lives. With this regenerative work, the goal of
which is nothing less ambitious than the worldwide exporting of
mental health (that is: spiritual and emotional well-being), we re-
store to ourselves and to our posterity the opportunity of leading
fulfilling lives. Instead of erecting grotesque monuments to ego,
greed, and unsatisfiable lusts for power and domination—Khufu's
Great Pyramid, a devastating train of genocidal wars, and the poi-
soning of our water, land, and air—imagine a world in which the
highest status belongs to a legacy of human interrelationships, of
having raised to flourishing adulthood children and grandchil-
dren, whose boundaries and feelings are intact and inviolate, and
whose energies are free to be deployed in the enterprise of renew-
ing a common world.

Even as experience tilts in favor of such a world, there will
still be plenty of crucifixion to go around. Whether by accident or
design, all the drives and stratagems of what André Malraux once
termed "the beast within us" will still harbor its ancient grudge
against us; now we know that the human person alone possesses
the power to tame that beast.

> Humanism does not consist in saying: "No animal could
> do what we have done," but in declaring: "We have re-
> fused to do what the beast within us willed to do, and we
> wish to rediscover Man wherever we discover that which
> seeks to crush him to the dust."
>
> —Andre Malraux, *The Voices of Silence*, p. 642

For all we know, Nature or God may be able to produce a
world-class hater like Hitler, Stalin or Pol Pot *ex nihilo*, in which
case all our efforts toward true salvation are forever doomed to fall
short of perfection. So what? Perfection was always an idle dream
of dilettantes and time-servers, tourists and exiles on earth, which

were merely passing through but never really got to know us or, in the end, cared much for our struggle.

Imagine then a world in which every individual has the opportunity to live out his life to the fullest, to pursue his wildest dreams and projects to the extent that it is possible to realize them in the world of men, women, and children, and the freedom to fail repeatedly without fear of ostracism and ignominy. Imagine a world of continuous, cradle-to-grave support (rather than manipulative marketing!). Isn't this what historic capitalism of the eighteenth and nineteenth centuries proclaimed as its ultimate goal? "You *damn'* right it is, America!" as Bernie Mac might exclaim.

For a single individual like Jesus of Nazareth to have made the historic impact that he did in itself constitutes for all conceivable purposes a sufficient *resurrection of the body*. Precisely how a realization that the physical organism of this particular human has been deceased for two thousand years is supposed to denigrate or depreciate that accomplishment is beyond me; if anything, Jesus' achievement and immortality (relatively speaking, at least) is even greater because of this indisputable fact of his mortal nature.

In the decades, centuries, and millennia to come, human beings have a lot to catch up on; a lot of make-up work to do: creating safe cities and establishing harmonious relations between states and nations; restoring the natural environment to a pristine state; eradicating nuclear arms and weapons of mass destruction; creating an international political climate that fosters a scaling down of tensions; negotiating ancient hatreds and conflicts; managing population growth and securing safe natural resources of water, land, and air for generations to come—just to mention a few of the more obvious challenges. Nobody else can do these things for us. And we cannot do them alone.

7

Gods and Goddesses

> Next, we must beware of superstition, by which our minds are turned aside from the true God, and carried to and fro after a multiplicity of gods. Therefore, if we are contented with one God, let us call to mind what was formerly observed, that all fictitious gods are to be driven far away, and that the worship which he claims for himself is not to be mutilated.

—John Calvin, Institutes of the Christian Religion [329]

As Schopenhauer decried in *On the Fourfold Root of the Principle of Sufficient Reason*, Hegel and his followers ignored Kant's decisive victory over speculative metaphysics after only fifty or sixty years. Just as the inability to resuscitate the argument from design does not alleviate the need for religious meaning, so Flew's argument, however compelling, does not entirely eliminate every avenue of inquiry into substantive religious issues.

Once we understand the limitation imposed by Kant and Schopenhauer on all attempts to export reason to supersensuous realms as a *misuse* of reason, perpetrated in the hope of smuggling in a species of arcane cognition, Flew's argument seems almost beside the point. Something in human nature cries out for meaning, and in particular for that species of meaning supplied by traditional religious experience. Thinking and reason have a need for meaning, as Hannah Arendt recognized. The demands of religion are inseparable from the general domain of meaning. Religion is inextricably bound up with the whole of aesthetic experience.

I will not broach here the topic of Plato's theory of forms or Cartesian substance dualism, beyond the simple observation, *en passant*, that its sway has been incalculable throughout the history of human thought. If Hannah Arendt correctly claims that "the two-world theory . . . is the most plausible delusion with which the experience of thought is plagued," then Plato was no less plagued by this "plausible delusion" than men before or after him—or, for that matter, than we are today. Belief in the soul is alluring, even when we reject any theological or religious suppositions arising out of Christianity; indeed, perhaps it is more alluring when we do so.

As to Descartes's first and third proofs of God's existence, Schopenhauer is once again instructive. Citing Aristotle's *Posterior Analytics*, he writes "the definition of a thing and the proof of its existence are two different and eternally separate matters" (p. 16). He goes on to quote Aristotle:

> *To be* does not belong to the essence of a thing, for existence is not an attribute or characteristic.

By calling existence a perfection, Descartes means precisely what Aristotle rules out; and premise 2 in both his first and third arguments is dealt a fatal blow. As Schopenhauer notes, this renowned philosopher and mathematician failed to properly distinguish *reasons*, or "grounds of knowledge," from *causes*, a failure shared with many philosophers, including Anselm and Aquinas.

That said, this particular criticism does not appear to touch Aquinas's Fourth Way, the "Moral" Argument (nor does it adequately cover Descartes's second proof, both of which I will consider in the next chapter).

New Age religions proclaim the Age of Aquarius and the Coming of the Goddess. Like all poets, I adore the feminine; but, like all poets and philosophers, I mistrust public relations;

therefore, I must confess to a small, unflinching resistance to the idea that we might simply reverse mythologies and mythopoeisis and blithely resume a goddess-centered polytheism. The whole idea is not without appeal, as Daniel Quinn explored in his remarkable novel, *The Holy*, and as millions of readers have found in Dan Brown's *Da Vinci Code*. Quinn's novel is, overall and in terms of its aesthetic quality, far superior to *Da Vinci*, particularly in its robust and honest treatment of the erotic and the supernatural. Brown's work is little more than a best-selling potboiler; well researched to be sure but more impressive for its marketing efficacy than for any enduring aesthetic or literary value.

A question—indeed, it is the central question of Quinn's novel, though not one that Brown ever gets around to posing—of some practical importance is: what ever happened to those old gods and goddesses of polytheism, deities and demons that the Israelites worshipped for centuries while evading the demands of their monotheistic landlord, Yahweh. The answer is: *nothing* happened to them. They are still out there. Flourishing. Accepting worship and rewarding their devotees with favors of all kinds.

Turn on the TV. Ever see Britney Spears back in the day? Celebrity sexpots, courtesans, and seductresses, from Marilyn Monroe and Liz Taylor to Jessica Alba and Rosario Dawson, and their male counterparts, from James Dean and Paul Newman to Brad Pitt and George Clooney have always participated in these deities, merging their human personas with their immortal natures. Magazine ads and billboards, movies and videos proclaim their sublime majesty, commending them as talismans worthy of emulation and worship. Their images attach to cars, clothing, jewelry, and food, banking, education, and insurance plans. Everywhere at once, provocatively commonplace and unseen, their potency survives in our sleeping desires and unconscious dreams, guiding our acts and choices along magic magnetic currents.

When Yahweh was busy exalting His Name and kicking the asses of all these minor polytheistic avatars, he was engaged in a massive marketing sweep and branding campaign; but he had no need to follow it up with deity-genocide. Annihilation was unnecessary; diminishing the aura of these lesser competitors was sufficient for advancing monotheism; after all, they were still minor deities. All Yahweh demanded was that He alone be deemed supremely worthy of worship. So, he banished them to a Phantom Zone of obloquy and irrelevance.

But, make no mistake, these deities still live and thrive, carving out little zones of dominion throughout the human world, where they can be worshipped and gratified, served and serviced; mixing and matching their motives and desires to our own. Romance and magic both exist, autonomous and real, as they always have: visible to their acolytes and trusted servants alone, who have the eyes to see and the ears to hear—invisible and silent to the rest of the world.

8

One True God

The words, "before me," go to increase the indignity, God being provoked to jealousy whenever we substitute our fictions in his stead; just as an unfaithful wife stings her husband's heart more deeply when her adultery is committed openly before his eyes.

—John Calvin, Institutes of the Christian Religion [329]

AQUINAS'S "MORAL" ARGUMENT FOR the existence of God does not confuse or conflate the definition of a thing with the proof of its existence, does not hypostatize any superfluous entity. The term, perfection, as employed in this argument, signifies nothing more than Aristotle's sense of an attributed quality or characteristic of a thing. If we review the argument through the lens of Descartes's second proof, the assertion of a "standard of perfection" merits our careful scrutiny.

René Descartes's second argument for God's existence in *Meditation 5* seems to turn on the notion that existence is a perfection; i.e., that the idea of God is such that I cannot imagine God without also imagining that God exists. This seems dubious until we read: "I ought still to regard the existence of God as having at least the same level of certainty as I have hitherto attributed to the truths of mathematics." The *rationale* here is: God exists in the same way that triangles, numbers, expansions, quadratic equations, or pure geometrical objects (or, for that matter, Platonic Forms) exist.

So, a second argument for God's existence may be extrapolated to run thus:

1. We may postulate an ideal standard against which to measure experience or knowledge.

2. To the extent that such an ideal standard is clear and distinct, it has reality if what is measured has reality.

It is axiomatic for Descartes that "God is no deceiver," for this is what undergirds the entire system of mathematical truths. An all-powerful God who wished to deceive us could undoubtedly permit us to hold "truths" of mathematics as mistakenly as beliefs that material objects were real. So, this "God is no deceiver" proposition in *Meditations One, Three, and Four* is a crucial part of Descartes's overall argument. It does not show that whatever beliefs we hold must be true; rather, it serves to assure us of hope that, if we persevere and stick to the outline of our master science, we will in the end arrive at propositions about which we are certain, or at least as certain as we can be.

By retaining Aristotle's distinction between *definition* and *proof of existence*, and that between Schopenhauer's *reason* and *cause*, we are able to salvage this much of Aquinas's "Moral" Argument, treating *perfection* as characteristic or quality of actual existing objects found in the external world, dropping the causal notion of *source* from Premise 4 and replacing it with *existence*. For standards of measurement, appraisal, and evaluation indisputably exist, standards of an objective and impartial kind.

Whether we wish to call such a standard of perfection God is beside the point; since, by definition, God is the source of all value; he contains all qualities, characteristics, and perfections to the highest possible degree. While this in no way allows us to hypostatize such an entity's existence in a material, empirical sense (i.e., as an additional object or creature in the universe), we can retain the notion as a "standard of perfection" or measurement in just the way outlined by Descartes. The only question is: what exactly, if anything, does our notion of God *measure*? And here, I believe, we are ineluctably thrown back on the central themes of this book.

So, Yahweh the monotheistic survivor of divine competition, rules supreme as the one true God. What does this mean for us and, in particular, for the contemporary and longstanding quandary of these co-existing multiple "major religions," all of which claim primary legitimacy and supreme authority?

Logically, if one accedes to the position of monotheism—at least historically inarguable—then clearly Christians, Jews, and Muslims worship numerically one and the same God, whatever names various natural languages may give to this entity. Probably the same can be said of Buddhism, Hinduism, and Taoism, to the extent that these ancient religious traditions assert a sovereign Godhead beyond the realm of sheer pantheism.

A synonymy among religious scriptures of these various sects authorizes us to go beyond such speculations and assert definitively that, if the Deity exists, then the teachings expressed throughout these various scriptures cannot contradict each other or be in actual disharmony. Jesus, Buddha, and Muhammad may be regarded, intellectually and spiritually, as almost a single person, their teachings a univocal expression of divine will desiring our collective and individual redemption. Such an interpretation has immense practical value, besides being enormously convenient to us humans.

"By their fruits you shall know them," is a Biblical maxim of sharp pragmatic import. When applied to our reflections on the multiplicity and often-antagonized conflictive relationships between and among the various sects of major religions, this saying's significance is quickly apparent. For this maxim is also a bona fide test of the authenticity of putative authority, permitting us to separate legitimate spiritual exemplars and living "saints" from braying demagogues and slick charlatans. "Distrust all," Friedrich Nietzsche acknowledges, "in whom the impulse to punish is powerful." Anybody, for instance, who is set too keenly, either in judgments propounded or policies advocated, on condemning and punishing "disbelievers" and "heretics" or who is too harshly sweeping in assigning blame for the various waves of evil and criminality that intermittently seem to flood the world—such persons we may disregard and dispense with altogether as unworthy of our consideration in the context of discussion and debate. We may gently remind them of Nietzsche's prudent warning before waving them aside, insisting that they take John Calvin's advice and devote themselves to actively listening to the better discourse of their brothers and sisters.

Islamist fanatics and jihadists, like their Judeo-Christian ideological counterparts, have no scriptural authority and can legitimately claim none. But the political and economic context of their contemporary existence cannot be ignored or overlooked any more than we can afford to deny or neglect the historical, cultural, and psychological circumstances and background conditions in which such aberrant tragedies as suicide-bombers have become a routine feature of the mundane world. Terrorists and psychopathic extremists did not become this way entirely of their own accord and all by themselves, out of the sheer perversity of abundant free will; there are reasons for the existence of Al-Qaeda as there are for the IRA and "School of the Americas" (euphemistically renamed the "Western Hemisphere Institute for Security Cooperation" for marketing reasons!), infamous for having trained most of the Third World's death squads.

We can no longer afford to neglect the contextual conditions of betrayal, disenfranchisement, and poverty, whether of the Middle East and Africa, Latin America, Eastern Europe, and Asia, or closer to home in the USA. Nor can we hope to simply wave a wand over ten thousand years of charismatic rulers, patriarchy, and paternalistic colonialism and expect to recreate our own idyllic mirror-concept of democracy and freedom. There are no "marginal people" in this world; those we banish to such a status will explode in headlines and images on our TV sets, LED screens, laptops, and smart phones. But at last, we have the power to alter this situation and our future.

If the peaceful redistribution and allocation of the world's material and human resources is the great economic challenge facing mankind in the twenty-first century, then a new and abiding spirituality will also be required to harmonize relationships among peoples and states and to harness diplomacy to effective strategies. Across a multiplicity of differing tongues and customs, against a whirlwind of fears, desires and demonic specters, and within a deluge of conflicting media opinions, information and threats, men, women, and children of good will and bright imagination must come together in doubt and fear to build bridges of communication from which a new and more durable world may be launched. No master blueprint of experts and no technical imperative can arbitrate this great nexus and renaissance. It will be by halting steps, amid confusion and terror, that the exemplars of courage and wisdom reveal themselves to the generations. On every side of the globe, actors will telescope into spectators, merging on a pilgrim's highway as they listen for an answering call.

It is the laughing call of an infant we will hear: the cry of an infant child in an earthly manger that must at last drown out those anguished cries of pain from a cross of our human fabrication.

9

America and Morality

> In another place Augustine uses these words, "Every good work in us is performed only by grace" (August. Ep. 105) ... "We know that Divine grace is not given to all men, and that to those to whom it is given, it is not given either according to the merit of works, or according to the merit of the will, but by free grace: in regard to those to whom it is not given, we know that the not giving of it is a just judgment from God" (August, ad Bonifac. Ep. 106).
>
> —John Calvin, *Institutes of the Christian Religion* [264]

WE ARE NOW IN a position to address the chief subject of these reflections: America's role in recent history and her responsibility for the future. I can at last drop my *ad hoc persona* of practical theologian and return to a more familiar one, namely: that of poet and seer. I pointedly do not speak of America's "destiny" because I would not leave my people or my world to anything so fortuitous as fate. But Fortuna is a powerful goddess, if notoriously fickle; I do not underestimate the sway of her command.

Contrary to Schopenhauer and Flew, there is "consciousness of God" as there is of the sublime and beautiful in literature, painting, music, and architecture—even politics. George Orwell may have suspected Gandhi as a crypto-totalitarian demagogue, but Gandhi proved his worth (as did Dr. Martin Luther King Jr., Malcolm X, President Lyndon Johnson, and Surgeon General C. Everett Koop). While such consciousness can never lead to cognition or knowledge in the sense of empirical science, it can lead us to an apprehension of the divine in a way that informs our sensibility and augments our judgment.

The evolving body of disciplinary knowledge pertaining to religion and theology is itself, like the concepts, history, material substance, and traditions inherent in that discipline, an empirical matter subject to investigation. Whatever informs, enhances or increases our awareness and judgment is itself intellectual knowledge. We do well not to shun, ignore or disparage that legacy and heritage.

America faces extraordinary contests and must soon make a number of awesome social decisions: about drug policy and education, about vital interests and intelligence, about employment and immigration, about environment and regulatory strategy governing corporate and scientific interests, about military posture and aging population, about diplomacy and international relations, defense and security. First and foremost among these, America will have to decide whether she wants to assume a continued role of leadership in the world for the duration of this transition—or stand back (perhaps as a consultant to the community of nations) while a European Union, China or confederation of autonomous communities plays that part. The geopolitical world of Winston Churchill's day has all but vanished: only the remnants of ancient ethnic hatreds and conspiracies remain like hungry ghosts; the world whose dimming boundaries these specters inhabit has changed beyond all recognition—or nearly so.

While I incline toward faith in humans, I have too much respect for our political life to believe that such struggles and decisions will flow harmoniously toward the future, or that progress is assured. The course of the transformation envisioned in these pages is, on the contrary, likely to be filled with bitter resistance, confrontation, and bloodshed—particularly if America has anything to say about it. Even if the bloodshed is, as I hope it will be, only metaphorical.

"We are circumscribed by the questions we ask." I am no doubt hampered by my Calvinist heritage, which sees in the autonomy of individual churches a dignity and deeply democratic power, communities capable of transforming the world and hearts of mortals. Such communities are far from infallible; many have no doubt inflicted immeasurable harm by stubbornly adhering to ideologically driven causes and by wreaking disfiguring schisms. For anyone who holds religious meaning to be sacred, the sectarian heresies, inquisitions, witch-hunts, and religious wars of several centuries are nothing to brag about. Nothing I have said in these pages about religion or the religious life can be taken as a defense of such disastrous blunders.

That anyone could complain about "godless atheists" the way certain Americans have throughout our history is but one more testament to entrenched ignorance. The redundancy is telling: all atheists are godless—by definition. That is what atheists believe: that no super-beings, no gods of any kind exist. Or perhaps they believe that no gods exist . . . *outside the human imagination*. All atheists hold that the universe itself is sacred and worthy of reverence. *A-theism*, properly speaking, is an ancient and highly respectable religious view, the view of atomists like Democritus and Lucretius.

My suggestions about the ubiquity of religious community and institutional churches throughout the world offering a glimmer of hope should not be misconstrued or over-interpreted. The organized Protestant and Catholic churches in America did nothing to address chattel slavery in the nineteenth century or Vietnam in the twentieth; indeed, such institutions showed a unique propensity for silence and neglect, and for staying oblivious to the needs of the nation and her people. Yet, in the lives of ordinary individuals at the level of neighborhood, community, and church, I have faith in the democratic instinct, moral quirkiness, and idiosyncratic humanity of my peers and fellow citizens, whose power to do good in the long run will triumph over obstacles of vanity, deceit, and self-serving stratagems. It is hard to say or even to speculate precisely how human engagement may be served by the explosion of online caring communities—or to imagine what new alliances and polities ordinary people of this world may conceive and create, much less the enterprises they may advance. Internet porn, child predators, and neo-Nazi groups get all the attention at present; yet these are a drop in the bucket compared to the millions and hundreds of millions of souls seeking communication and friendship across the planet.

> Once Jesus was asked by the Pharisees when the kingdom of God was coming, and he answered, 'The kingdom of God is not coming with things that can be observed; nor will they say, "Look, here it is!" or "There it is!" For, in fact, the kingdom of God is among you.'

Appendix I
Classic Proofs of God's Existence

THERE ARE SIX BASIC arguments that have been employed traditionally to argue to a conclusion that something like a deity or god exists. These are:

1. The "Ontological" Argument

2. The "Prime Mover" Argument

3. The "First Cause" Argument

4. The "Cosmological" Argument

5. The "Moral" Argument

6. The "Teleological" or "Design" Argument

While these may not be the only arguments for the existence of God, they are the oldest and best known. Since these arguments may be indefinitely varied in terms of their specific presentation, it is perhaps worth studying them first. The first argument, the "Ontological" argument, is credited to St. Anselm, a medieval philosopher and theologian. It is the best-known deductive argument for God's existence and, although widely recognized as deductively valid, it is equally widely held to fail to establish God's existence as a factual, empirical truth, a knowable matter.

1. The Ontological Argument

P-1 God is a being than which none greater can be conceived.

P-2 That which exists in reality is greater than that which exists only in thought.

P-3 If God does not exist in reality, then He exists only as an object of thought.

P-4 If God exists only as an object of thought, then one can conceive of a being greater than God (namely: a God who exists both in reality and as an object of thought).

P-5 If God exists only as an object of thought, then God is not a being than which none greater can be conceived.

P-6 Therefore, if God is a being than which none greater can be conceived, then God cannot be conceived of as not existing.

Conclusion: Therefore, God necessarily exists.

The next group of arguments, known collectively as the "Five Ways," is the invention of Thomas Aquinas, a very great medieval philosopher and the source of the scholastic canon of the Roman Catholic Church known as Thomism. These are arguments whose appeal rests largely on some feature or features ostensibly empirical in nature; or so we shall regard them.

2. The First Way: Prime Mover

P-1 All things move and change.

P-2 This is easily observed all around us.

P-3 All things come into being, develop, and eventually cease to exist.

P-4 None of these things bring themselves into existence.

Conclusion: A first, or prime, mover must exist which began this whole process, which we call God.

3. The Second Way: First Cause

P-1 All sensible things have causes.

P-2 No sensible thing causes itself.

P-3 This is easily witnessed all around us.

Conclusion: A first, or prime, cause must exist which began this whole process, and this first cause we call God.

4. The Third Way: The Cosmological Argument

P-1 If all being were contingent, then we could infer an antecedent time when nothing existed.

P-2 Creation *ex nihilo* [out of nothing] is impossible.

P-3 Therefore it is not the case that all being is contingent.

P-4 Therefore some being is non-contingent, or necessary.

Conclusion: A necessary being exists, which we call God.

5. The Fourth Way: The Moral Argument

P-1 All things possess degrees of qualities and perfections.

P-2 This is true of all values and qualities such as goodness, beauty, truth, nobility, courage, heat, cold and so forth.

P-3 We can say whether a particular thing possesses a quality to a greater or lesser degree.

P-4 From this we may infer the source of a perfect standard with respect to all of these qualities.

Conclusion: Such a standard of perfection exists, which we call God.

6. *The Fifth Way: The Teleological argument*

[Argument from Design]

P-1   There are innumerable instances of purposive order to be seen throughout the universe [1. salmon swimming upstream to the place of their birth in order to spawn; 2. the fact that any one of us might be motivated by some future event (promotion; earning a degree; getting an "A" in a course) to study in the present; 3. the "fitness" of our environment in supplying us with nourishing food. . .N].

P-2   There could not be such innumerable instances of purposive order unless there was also an intelligent designer.

Conclusion: An Intelligent Designer exists, which we call God.

Besides the arguments of Anselm and Aquinas, the seventeenth-century philosopher and mathematician, Rene Descartes, devised three proofs purportedly as proof of God's existence.

Descartes's Proofs of God's Existence

First Proof:

P-1   I have an idea of God, an infinite and perfect being.

P-2   There must be as much reality in the cause of an idea as there is in the content of the idea.

P-3   I could not possibly be the source of my idea of God.

P-4   Only God could be the source of my idea of God.

P-5   Therefore, God exists.

Second Proof:

P-1   I exist as a thing that has an idea of God.

P-2   Every existent has a cause that brought it into existence and that sustains it in existence.

P-3   The only thing adequate to cause and sustain me, a thing that has an idea of God, is God.

P-4   Therefore, God exists.

Third Proof:

P-1   My conception of God is the conception of a being that possesses all perfections.

P-2   Existence is a perfection.

P-3   Therefore I cannot conceive of God as not existing.

P-4   Therefore, God exists.

Appendix II
A Primer of Logic & Epistemology
[Theory of Knowledge]

IN WHAT FOLLOWS, I have condensed the cumulative training of more than twenty-five years into a handful of basic tools, which will help you begin what I truly hope will be a lifelong love of learning based on the pursuit of truth, knowledge and wisdom. Good luck to you!

Prospective Logic Student's Question: Why should I bother to study logic?
Logic Teacher's Answer: What argument shall I use to convince you?

Logic is the study of reasoning and argumentation, with a view to constructing arguments that are both *valid [have the correct structure]* and *sound [correct structure and true conclusion],* and to distinguishing these from flawed or *fallacious* arguments. Both as a formal discipline and a practical activity, logic is closely connected to another branch of philosophy called epistemology or theory of knowledge, which is concerned with the nature of knowledge and what is knowable. For this reason, logic is more than "the backbone of philosophy," as Bertrand Russell called it; the study of logic is intimately connected with human nature and every aspect of human life, activities and society, including psychology, education, family, politics, law and criminal justice, religion, artistic creation and scientific investigation. Because logic is concerned with matters of fact at the level of definition, it may be thought of as fundamental, i.e., as a *requirement* for effectively pursuing every other discipline and activity, and particularly for adequately and responsibly discharging one's *duties as a citizen.*

In the study of logic, an *argument* is not the unpleasant squabbling or heated contest of wills we sometimes experience with parents and siblings, peers and co-workers. For logicians, an *argument* is simply a set of *assertions* or *propositions* purporting to lead to a *conclusion* (whether they do or not is something to be determined by an analysis and evaluation). A *proposition* is any assertion that is, or can be, either true or false. A word or a phrase is not a sentence. The phrase "in a garden" or "Felix's hat" for example is not a sentence. But "A + B = C" is. So is the following formula from

$$\exists(x)\ (Fx \to Gx)$$

which asserts that there is at least $\exists$ one individual x such that *IF* x has the property F *THEN* x has the property G (for example: Some frogs are green).

There are two basic kinds of argument: *Deductive* and *Inductive*. An *argument* is held to be *deductively valid* if and only if, given that its premises are true, the *conclusion* cannot be false [Definition 1]. Notice that this definition of validity says nothing about whether the conclusion of a purportedly valid deductive argument is true; as a matter of fact, it may not be. This allows us to distinguish the difference between a merely valid argument and a sound one. A deductively valid argument in which the conclusion is also true is said to be a *sound argument* [Definition 2]. Let's consider some pertinent examples:

> All S is P.
>
> Some M is S.
>
> Some M is P.

I have borrowed this form of argument, called a *syllogism*, from the ancient Greek philosopher, Aristotle. Many philosophers credit Aristotle with the discovery or invention of formal logic as a discipline. Aristotle's syllogisms admitted only four forms of statement: Universal Affirmative [All S is P], Universal Denial [No S is P], Existential Affirmative [Some S is P] and Existential Denial [Some S is not-P]. But what do the terms S, P and M stand for? To flesh out the form of this *categorical syllogism*, we will need to assign some values to these predicate letters. If we let S = Men, P = Mortal, M = Socrates, we get a particular instance of this argument form:

Premise 1	All men are mortal.
Premise 2	Socrates is a man.
Conclusion	Socrates is mortal.

The two premises are sufficient to support the conclusion, which appears to follow from the combined premises; and the conclusion is true. This argument is deductively valid and is strictly analogous to the following mathematical argument:

$$A + B = C$$

But suppose we let S = bats, P = cats and M = Monteverdi. The argument becomes:

P-1	All bats are cats
P-2	Monteverdi is a bat
Conclusion	Monteverdi is a cat

In this instance, even while the argument form is deductively valid, at least one premise, the Universal Affirmative [P-1] is false, which makes the premise set [P-1 + P-2] insufficient to support the conclusion, which may or may not be true.

Since our discussion of support has broached the subject of *evidence*, we may do well to examine the notions of *rational* and *empirical* knowledge.

Consider this argument: If A is less than B, B less than C, then A is less than C.

$$((A < B) + (B < C)) \rightarrow (A < C)$$

Here the arrow stands for the *IF . . .THEN* relation, otherwise known as the logical connective, *implication*. The argument embodied by this sentence or *proposition* looks straightforwardly deductive; what is more, it is true no matter what values are assigned to interpret A, B and C. Such a form is called a *tautology* and is true under any interpretation.

Consider the following propositions:

The square root of 4 is 2.

A bachelor is an unmarried man.

This sleeping pill works because of its soporific properties.

What makes these claims true, if they are true? These claims are true by definition, tautologies, as are the truths of mathematics. Such truths are called, by turns, *rational, necessary, deductive,* or *analytic,* and represent knowledge that is known *a priori* (from the Latin, meaning that it is known "prior to" or independent of any particular sensory experience). This is roughly analogous to the kind of knowledge that Bertrand Russell called "knowledge by description." Such truths seem self-evident and may provide reasons for our holding particular beliefs to be true or false.

But there is another kind of knowledge, variously called *empirical, contingent, inductive,* and *synthetic,* which is known *a posteriori* (once again from the Latin, meaning the kind of knowledge that follows from, or is dependent upon, sensory experience).

Take, for example, these propositional claims:

Goats breathe through their ears.

Water suffocates.

Aspirin kills cats.

Such things as these sentences claim cannot be known a priori, as a matter of the definition of terms. To know whether an empirical claim is true, we must investigate some aspect of physical nature (goat anatomy, biology, and physiology, in the case of the first claim). Empirical investigation often involves the discovery of *causes*, something that lies at the heart of the scientific enterprise. The Scottish philosopher, David Hume, believed that nothing could be known a priori about causes. Rational truth Hume called knowledge of "relations of ideas"; empirical truths he termed "matters of fact." Hume is a quintessential empiricist.

Immanuel Kant, an equally great philosopher and a contemporary of Hume's, argued persuasively that what we call modern science involves both kinds of truth (i.e., rational and empirical). Kant distinguished a phenomenal realm or realm of appearance, governed by a deterministic law of causality (i.e., cause-and-effect), roughly correlated with Hume's sensory realm, from a noumenal realm (from Latin *noumena*, meaning mind or intellect), which Kant thought of as the underlying reality behind appearances. [*Note: Kant believed that there was one world or universe, but thought he could distinguish these two realms for the purpose of explanation.]

In this noumenal realm, human actions are governed by a "law of freedom" identical to the moral law, no mere appearance but the "thing-in-itself"!

Hume offered this account of causality:

1)   A and B are joined with one another in space and time. ("No action at a distance.")

2)   B follows A. (The "effect" does not precede the "cause")

_____

3)   Whenever A occurs, B occurs; and vice-versa ("constant conjunctions")

Statement 3 falls far short of a causally sufficient condition or a deterministic cause. If we directly observe only 1 and 2, what real basis could we have for making such an inference? If all we have is mere juxtaposition—i.e., constant conjunction—of two events, what happens to the vaunted "law of causality"?

In Hume's view, all three of these relationships may be observed in any two events that are only coincidentally connected with one another. For example, a flash of lightning occurs and Jones falls dead. Surely, the lightning flash did not cause Jones's death; yet, Hume insists that every imputed instance of cause-and-effect has no better claim on our cognition than this. Consequently,

Hume reasoned: we have no knowledge about cause-and-effect, only constant conjunction.

When we say that "All husbands must be married" is true by definition, we patently do not mean that "All husbands have been irresistibly forced into marriage." When Hume asks in a famous essay,

> "What is the foundation of all our reasonings concerning cause and effect, underlying all our experience?"

he unequivocally answers: It is nothing more or less than convention, custom or habit.

Custom or Convention (Habit)

(1)   All observed Cs are or have been Fs.

(2)   All Cs have been, are, and will be Fs.

For Hume, Statement (1) is the basis for our belief in Statement (2); but this is no guarantee of the certainty of Statement 2. Let's symbolize this causal relation as P→R, interpreting Hume's conventional inference with the familiar "Whatever will be, will be." Hume's answer to the question, "Will the future be like the past?" might be translated by

$$(P \to R) \to (P \to R)$$

which looks rather like a logical, truth-functional relation, the truth of which does not depend on the values we ascribe to P and R; in other words: a tautology.

> Whatever will be, will be.
> (X will be) → (X will be).

The whole sentence is a valid inference as a demand of logical necessity, since anything follows from itself by the law of identity. But this does not mean that the whole sentence is instantiated—out there, somehow—in the world.

Let us unpack some distinct causal notions. We will use the token of equivalence ≡ to indicate a *definition*.

> Necessary Cause ≡ Without F, Y will not occur.
>
> Sufficient Cause ≡ Whenever F occurs, Y must occur, too.

Where F is a prior event and Y is a later event:

A somewhat different concept is that of a *probabilistic, statistical* or *inductive* cause, which may be defined thus: When A occurs, it increases the probability or likelihood that B will occur.

We must carefully distinguish *reasons* from *causes*. While some proposition p might provide a reason for holding some particular belief H, p does not cause H. When stated plainly and clearly, this seems obvious and absurd; yet, we often confuse the two notions. The terms "logical" and "common-sense" are often used interchangeably, as virtual synonyms. Every day one can hear someone assert, like the Vulcan Spock in *Star Trek*, that some course of action "is not logical." Such bald assertions are rarely (if ever) followed by citation of specific fallacies, weaknesses in support or reasoning. No reference is ever made to definitions, arguments, premises, conclusion, validity and soundness during these displays and this is not surprising: even among the well educated, few persons bother to study logic, formally or informally. I suspect the attribution of "not logical" is most often nothing more than code for the attributor's disagreement with an opponent's position. Hand waving does not constitute argument; in most cases, this amounts to nothing less than a false and shallow charge of fallacy, which, when unsubstantiated, itself constitutes a serious and often fatal fallacy of reasoning.

Conclusion:

Every argument is empirical to just the degree that it is substantive (i.e., about something); and all substantive arguments probably have dimensions that are both rational and deductive, on the one hand, as well as empirical and inductive, on the other. This does not mean we can dispense with formal tools of assessment; rather, it suggests that we must bring both deductive and inductive considerations to bear on every argument in order to effectively evaluate its merits. As Charles Peirce noted more than a century ago in his wonderful essay, "The Fixation of Belief," most persons search for arguments only to further reinforce the beliefs they hold by virtue of "tenacity," regardless of the respective merits, truth or falsity of those beliefs. Still others construct arguments and select reasons only to justify the a priori ideals to which they are already committed, ideals untroubled and untainted by empirical evidence.

The fact that a person may present an argument whose premises are sloppy, erroneous and fallacious—premises that do not support the conclusion, either deductively or inductively—yet whose particular conclusion is nonetheless true, is not an invitation to forgo the study of logic, as if it were some luxury we can do without. We should not ignore the truth, even if adequately defining truth proves elusive, as Socrates taught us long ago. There is no duty to neglect the truth. Unless we intend to march into the future as willing slaves, we do have a duty to master the tools of logical study to the best of our ability, so that we might bring them to bear on the hard task of understanding the arguments we confront in our daily lives as persons and citizens, in order to meet the challenge of assessing those arguments on their actual merits—rather than whims of advertisers, prejudice of pundits, or agendas of the powerful.

Bibliography

IN A DISCURSIVE, NOT to say personal, essay, the requirements of scholarship are misplaced; there is no need for footnotes, citations of sources; and I have kept these to a minimum. But even a partial bibliography of references may be helpful to readers. The list below consists mostly of books I have read in their entirety: certainly Arendt, the two Millers, Eliade and Ricoeur, Tillich, and Bonhoeffer. I have relied on the Revised Standard Edition of The Holy Bible for scriptural citations and a 1989 one-volume edition of John Calvin's *Institutes of the Christian Religion*, available online. While I had not read Hauer and Young's *An Introduction to the Bible: A Journey into Three Worlds*, I recently purchased the eighth edition (Pearson Education, 2012).

Owen Barfield's works are incisive and highly relevant, particularly *Poetic Diction* and *Saving the Appearances: A Study in Idolatry*. Of similar merit are the essays in Howard Nemerov's *Figures of Thought: Speculations on the Meaning of Poetry & Other Essays* (Boston: David R. Godine, 1978), especially "Exceptions and Rules," "On the Resemblances Between Science and Religion," "Poetry and Meaning," "Speaking Silence," and "What Was Modern Poetry? Three Lectures."

All manner of resources pertaining to history of religion, theology and mysticism are widely available via the internet. Detailed bibliographies for each of the major figures listed below can be found online at Wikipedia, including numerous hyperlinks to works in the public domain or available for purchase. I have relied

on Wikipedia for some of the following bibliographic information. There is as well a vastly comprehensive knowledge base and detailed online bibliography of religion and theology at:
http://www.davidcox.com.mx/library/library.htm

The Holy Bible: Revised Standard Edition. New York: Thomas Nelson & Sons, 1946 (Revised 1952, 1959, 1971). There are online versions of the New Revised Standard Edition of the Bible at:
http://www.devotions.net/bible/oobible.htm and
http://bible.oremus.org/

Arendt, Hannah. *Between Past and Future*. London: Faber & Faber, 1961.

———*Crisis of the Republic*. New York: Harcourt, 1972.

———*Eichmann in Jerusalem: A Report on the Banality of Evil*. London: Faber & Faber, 1963.

———*The Human Condition*. Chicago: University of Chicago Press, 1958.

———*The Life of the Mind*, One-Volume Edition. New York: Harcourt Brace Jovanovich, 1978.

———*Lectures on Kant's Political Philosophy*. Brighton: Harvester, 1982.

———*Men in Dark Times*. New York: Harcourt Brace Jovanovich, 1968.

———*On Revolution*. New York: Penguin, 1962.

———*On Violence*. New York: Harcourt Brace Jovanovich, 1970.

Ausmus, Harry J.. *The Polite Escape: On the Myth of Secularization*. Athens: Ohio University Press, 1982.

Barfield, Owen. *History in English Words*. Hudson, New York: Lindisfarne, 1986.

———*Poetic Diction: A Study in Meaning*. Middletown, Connecticut: Wesleyan University Press, 1973.

———*The Rediscovery of Meaning, and Other Essays*. Middletown, Connecticut: Wesleyan University Press, 1979.

———*Saving the Appearances*. New York: Harcourt, Brace and World, 1965.

Bonhoeffer, Dietrich. *Ethics*. London: SCM, 1955.

———*Ethics* [critical edition]. Edited by Clifford Green. Translated by Krauss, Reinhard, Douglas W. Stott, and Charles C. West. Minneapolis, Minnesota: Fortress, 2004.

Brett, R. L., and A. R. Jones, eds. *Lyrical Ballads Wordsworth and Coleridge. The text of the 1798 edition with the additional 1800 poems*. New York: Barnes & Noble, 1963.

Brown, Norman O. "Apocalypse: The Place of Mystery in the Life of the Mind." In *Interpretation: The Poetry of Meaning*. Edited by Hopper, S. R. and D. L. Miller. New York: Harcourt Brace and World, 1967.

Calvin, John. *Institutes of the Christian Religion* [A one-volume edition]. Translated by Henry Beveridge. Grand Rapids, Michigan: Wm. B. Eerdmans, 1989.

DeMause, Lloyd. *The History of Childhood: The Untold Story of Child Abuse.* New York: Peter Bedrick, 1988.

Eliade, Mircea. *Images and Symbols: Studies in Religious Symbolism,* Translated by P. Mairet. London: Harvill, 1961.

———*Myth and Reality.* Translated by Willard R. Trask. New York: Harper and Row, 1963.

———*The Quest: History and Meaning in Religion.* London: University of Chicago Press, 1969.

———*The Sacred and the Profane: The Nature of Religion.* Translated from French by Willard R. Trask. New York: Harcourt Brace & World, 1963.

———*Symbolism, the Sacred, and the Arts.* Edited by Diane Apostolos-Cappadona. New York: The Crossroad, 1986.

Fehrenbacher, Don E., ed. *Abraham Lincoln Speeches and Writings 1859–1865.* New York: The Library of America. 1989.

Flew, Antony. "Theology and Falsification," Oxford: *University,* 1950. http://www.infidels.org/library/modern/antony_flew/theologyandfalsification.html and www.stephenjaygould.org/ctrl/flew_falsification.html

Freud, Sigmund. *Civilization and Its Discontents.* Translated by James Strachey. New York: W. W. Norton, 1989.

———*The Future of an Illusion.* New York: W. W. Norton, 1989.

———*Moses and Monotheism.* Translated by Katherine Jones. New York: Vintage, 1955.

Gates, John A. *Christendom Revisited; a Kierkegaardian View of the Church Today.* Philadelphia: Westminster, 1963.

———*The Life and Thought of Kierkegaard for Everyman.* Philadelphia: Westminster, 1960.

Hauer, Christian E., and William A. Young. *An Introduction to the Bible: A Journey into Three Worlds.* 6th edition. New York: Prentice Hall, 2005.

Jung, C. G. "Transformation Symbolism in the Mass," in Eranos Yearbooks, Vol. 2: The Mysteries. New York: Pantheon, 1955.

Kant, Immanuel. *Religion within the Limits of Bare Reason.* Jonathan Bennett, 2017. https://www.earlymoderntexts.com/assets/pdfs/kant1793.pdf

Malraux, André. *The Voices of Silence.* Translated by Stuart Gilbert. Princeton: Princeton University Press, 1978.

Miles, T. R. *Speaking of God: Theism, Atheism and the Magnus Image.* York: William Sessions, 1998.

Miller, Alice. *Banished Knowledge: Facing Childhood Injuries.* New York: Anchor, 1991.

———*Breaking Down the Wall of Silence: The Liberating Experience of Facing Painful Truth.* Translated by Simon Worral. New York: Meridian, 1997.

———*The Drama of the Gifted Child: The Search for the True Self.* Translated by Ruth Ward. New York: Basic, 1997.

———*For Your Own Good: Hidden Cruelty in Child-Rearing and the Roots of Violence.* New York: Farrar, Straus, Giroux, 1983.

————*Pictures of a Childhood: Sixty-six Watercolors and an Essay*. Translated by Hildegarde Hannum. Collingdale, Pennsylvania: Diane, 1999.

————*Thou Shalt Not Be Aware: Society's Betrayal of the Child*. New York: Farrar, Straus, Giroux, 1984.

————*The Untouched Key: Tracing Childhood Trauma in Creativity and Destructiveness*. Translated by Hunter Hannum. New York: Doubleday, 1990.

Miller, Perry. *The American Transcendentalists, their Prose and Poetry*. Garden City: Doubleday, 1957.

————*Consciousness in Concord: The Text of Thoreau's Hitherto "Lost Journal*. Boston: Houghton Mifflin, 1958.

————*Errand into the Wilderness*. Cambridge: Harvard University Press, 1956.

————*Jonathan Edwards*. New York: W. Sloane Associates, 1949.

————*The New England Mind: The Seventeenth Century*. New York: Macmillan, 1939.

————*The New England Mind: From Colony to Province*. Cambridge: Harvard University Press, 1953.

————*Orthodoxy in Massachusetts, 1630–1650*. Cambridge: Harvard University Press, 1933.

————*The Raven and the Whale: Poe, Melville and the New York Literary Scene*. Baltimore: The Johns Hopkins University Press, 1997.

————*The Responsibility of Mind in a Civilization of Machines: Essays by Perry Miller*. Amherst: The University of Massachusetts Press, 1979.

————*Roger Williams: His Contribution to the American Tradition*. New York: Atheneum, 1962.

————*The Life of the Mind in America: From the Revolution to the Civil War*. New York: Harcourt, Brace & World, 1965.

Niebuhr, Reinhold. *Moral Man and Immoral Society*. New York: Charles Scribner's Sons, 1932.

————*An Interpretation of Christian Ethics*. New York: Charles Scribner's Sons, 1935.

Otto, Rudolf. *The Idea of the Holy: An Inquiry into the Non Rational Factor in the Idea of the Divine 1926*. Translated by John W. Harvey. Whitefish, Montana: Kessinger, 2004.

Phillips, Dewi Zephaniah. *Religion and the Hermaneutics of Contemplation*. UK: Cambridge University Press, 2001.

Quinn, Daniel. *Ishmael*. New York: Random House, 1992.

————*The Holy*. Context, 2004.

Ricoeur, Paul. *Fallible Man*. Translated with an introduction by Walter J. Lowe. New York: Fordham University Press, 1986.

————*The Symbolism of Evil*. Translated by Emerson Buchanan. New York: Harper and Row, 1967 (1960).

————*Freud and Philosophy: An Essay on Interpretation*. Translated by Denis Savage. New Haven: Yale University Press, 1970.

————*The Rule of Metaphor: Multi-Disciplinary Studies in the Creation of Meaning in Language,* Translated by Robert Czerny with Kathleen McLaughlin and John Costello, S. J., London: Routledge and Kegan Paul, 1978.

————*Time and Narrative (Temps et Récit).* Translated by Kathleen McLaughlin and David Pellauer. Chicago: University of Chicago Press, 1984, 1985, 1988.

Schopenhauer, Arthur. *On the Fourfold Root of the Principle of Sufficient Reason.* Translated from the German by E. F. J. Payne. Introduction by Richard Taylor. La Salle, Illinois: Open Court, 1974.

Stebbing, Paul. *A Rat's Art.* Kansas City, Missouri: Scrimshaw Press, 2007.

Tillich, Paul. *The Protestant Era.* Chicago: University of Chicago Press, 1948. https://archive.org/details/protestantera009841mbp/page/n7

————*The Shaking of the Foundations.* New York: Charles Scribner's Sons, 1948.

————*Systematic Theology Volume 1: 1951–63.* Chicago: University of Chicago Press, 1951.

————*Volume 2: Existence and the Christ.* Chicago: University of Chicago Press, 1957.

————*Volume 3: Life and the Spirit: History and the Kingdom of God.* Chicago: University of Chicago Press, 1963.

————*The Courage to Be.* 2nd edition. New Haven: Yale University Press, 1952.

————*Dynamics of Faith.* New York: Harper and Row, 1957.

Tolstoy, Leo. *The Death of Ivan Ilyitch & Other Stories.* New York: Barnes & Noble Classics, 2004.

Van der Leeuw, Gerardus. *Sacred and Profane Beauty: The Holy in Art.* New York: Holt, Rinehart and Winston, 1963.

Van Buren, Paul. *The Secular Meaning of the Gospel.* New York: Macmillan, 1969.

Weber, Max. *The Protestant Work Ethic and the Spirit of Capitalism.* New York: Routledge Classics, 1992. Available online at: http://www.ne.jp/asahi/moriyuki/abukuma/weber/world/ethic/pro_eth_frame.html

Wills, Gary. *What Jesus Meant.* New York: Viking. 2006.

————*What Paul Meant.* New York: Viking. 2006.

Wittgenstein, Ludwig. *Zettel.* Anscombe, Elizabeth and von Wright, Georg Henrik, editors. Berkeley: University of California Press, 1975.

Index

A

A Christmas Carol, 38
A Portrait of the Artist as a Young Man, 23
a personal god, 28, 43, 47
a priori, 7, 56, 85, 86, 89
Abraham, 16, 27
Adam and Eve, 22
Adamic fall, 33
addiction, 29, 40, 41
aesthetic experience, 64
  and judgment, 65
  place in human affairs of, 27
  and scriptural literature, 35
Age of Aquarius, 64
AIDS Pandemic, 41
Alba, Jessica, 65
Amazon, 39
America
  complex religious tradition, 9–10, 13
  risks religious apostasy and political heresy, 11–12,15
  tortuous embrace of religiosity, 14
  skewed version of Christianity, 18
  obsession with materialism, 38
  "School of the Americas," 70
  role in history, destiny, 72

the transformation envisioned, 73–74
Anselm, 19, 77, 80
  "Ontological" Argument, 19, 20
  and reason-cause distinction, 64
Antigone, 31
Apostle's Creed, 14
Aquinas, Thomas
  "Five Ways," 18, 21, 78
  and "Argument from Design," 23
  and "Intelligent Design," 43
Aristotelian science, 21
  related to Descartes' arguments, 23, 67
Arendt, Hannah, 3, 4
  "God is Dead," 24
  Jesus and action, 29
  nature of evil, 33–34
  "need for meaning," dualism ("two-world" theory), 64
  concept of authority, 13
argument, 19, 88–89
  deductive argument defined, 19–20, 83
  inductive argument defined, 19, 21, 45, 85, 88, 89
Argument from Design, 5, 23–24, 63, 80
Aristotle
  logic and grammar, 19

Aristotle *(continued)*
  obsolete science, 21
  and mortality, 32, 60
  political life and community, 36
  on scientific proof (*Posterior
    Analytics*), 64, 67, 68
  inventor of formal logic, 83–84
atheists, atheism, 74
atonement (defined), 57
Augustine, 9, 72
Ausmus, Harry
  God with No Name, 24
  "the problem of God," 25, 43
authority
  personal, 1
  Roman origin, essentially
    political, 13
  traditional authority, legitimacy
    of, 53
  putative test of, 69

B

Ba'al, 18
Baghdad, 4
Bahai, 45
Bible, 4, 46
Biblical Genesis, 22
Biblical inerrancy, literalism, 51
Big Bang, 22
Blake, William, 29, 35
Boeing, 39
Bonhoeffer, Dietrich, 2
  Christ as standard for measur-
    ing human action, 49
  secularization as fulfillment of
    Christian eschatology, 59
Bread for the World, 40
Brown, Dan, 65
Brown, Norman O., 60
Buchan, William, 35
Buddha
  and compassion, 17, 54
Buridan's donkey, 38
Bush, George H. W., 4, 52
Bush, George W., 11, 52

business jargon, 38

C

Caesar, 39
Cain, 33
Calvin and Calvinism, 1, 74
  rejection of fervor, 8
  Calvin's maxim, 8, 10, 70
  and ethico-religious teleology, 9
capitalism
  and contingency, 36
  and utilitarianism, 34
  as chief vehicle of seculariza-
    tion, 38
  economic hegemony, 12
  created conditions of its own
    obsolescence, 39, 41
  and human nature, 40
  guaranteed full employment, 39
  Protestant secularism, 9
  new economic world described,
    62
  new economic foundation, 41
  defined by profit-maximization,
    41, 42
  peaceful redistribution of
    world's resources, 38–39, 71
  temple earth metaphor, 37,
    38, 42
  entrepreneurial Gospel of
    Wealth and Success, 17. *See
    also* marketing
causation, causality, 22, 51, 68,
  86–88
charisma, charismatic, 1, 15, 70
childhood, child development, 29
  natality, 28
  and innocence, 33
  "soul-murder," abuse of, 35, 41,
    46–48
  history of, 35–36, 36n
  and childhood selves, 61. *See
    also* Miller, Alice
childlike faith, 5

Christianity
  claims and doctrine of, 4
  three conceptual constellations,
    5
  and mysticism, world religions,
    45
  neo-Christians, "strict con-
    structionist" 17–18
church, churches
  and Vietnam, 2
  doctrine, 14
  and transnational corporations,
    12, 38
  autonomy and failures of, 74
Civil War, 15
civil war, 39
classic proofs of God's existence
  discussed, 18–19
  "Ontological" Argument, dis-
    cussed 19, 20, 77–78
  "Prime Mover," 21–22, 23, 78
  "First Cause" argument, 21–23,
    79
  "Cosmological" argument, 22,
    79
  "Moral" argument, 23, 24, 79
  "Teleological" or "Design" argu-
    ment, 23–24, 80
Clooney, George, 65
cognition, 8, 63, 86
community
  faith and identity of, 1, 8, 13
  and Anne Hutchinson, 15
  ultimate goal of, 28
  larger community, 36
  community of nations, 73
consciousness
  individual, and salvation, 27
  and collective, 33
  revolution in, 35
  for dignity, equality, 47
  and the standard of human
    action, 49
  and development of Western,
    60

apprehension of divine beauty,
    73
conservatives, 12, 17–18
"Contemporary Jewish Thought,"
    2
Cornford, F. M., 27
corporate
  excesses, profit-maximization,
    39
  fosters culture of cynicism and
    greed, 39
  entrepreneurial innovation, 40
  juggernaut, monoliths, hubris,
    48
  regulation of, 39
corporations
  extension of Mother Church,
    body of Christ, 12
  multinational and transna-
    tional, 12, 38, 41
Cotton, John, 14, 15
counterfactuals, 44, 45, 55
critical morality, 51–52
crucifixion, 60–61
culture
  advertising, 11
  marketing, 14, 16, 37
  American, 15, 32
  diversity of, 34
  changes in human, 36, 40
  industrial vs. service sector, 38

D

Da Vinci Code, 65
Daedalus, Stephen, 23
Darwinian evolution, 22
Dawson, Rosario, 65
Dean, James, 65
death, 4–5
  discussed, 31–35
  Hobbesian fear of, 27
  "cut off from God," 33
  central fact about religion, 31
  centrality to Jesus' life mission,
    17

death *(continued)*
death penalty, 53
death squads, 70
death-grip of indefensible views, 5
death-in-life, as sin, 33, 34, 35
distinguished from physical death, 32–33
ubiquity of, 32, 34. *See* "soul-murder"
deities, 65, 66
democracy
American context of, 34
how to advance, 40
colonialism's effect on, 70
DeMause, Lloyd, 36n3
Democritus, 74
deontology, 50
Descartes, Rene
three unique proofs, 18–19
borrows from Aquinas, 23, 24
existence a perfection, 64
second proof, discussion and extrapolated argument, 67–69
Second Proof, 81
Deus Absconditus, 18
Dickens, Charles, 38
divinity
concept and discussion, 47
phenomenology of, 48
standard of, 49
Doctors Without Borders, 40

E

economy, economics
hegemony of capitalism, 12
change required, 36
service sector global economics, Scylla and Charybdis of, 39
new economic world described, 39–42
the temple metaphor, 37, 38, 42
peaceful redistribution of world resources, 38, 71
new economic foundation, 41
egotism, hubris (as evil)
discussed, with examples, 52, 53, 54
Eliade, Mircea, 25
emotional fervor, 8
Emotional I.Q., 36
emotions, 8, 28, 52
empirical evidence, 20, 89
empirical investigation, 85
empirical science, 22, 45, 73
empirical statement, 44
empirical theory, 35
empirical truth, 46, 77, 86
enlightenment, 8
Enlightenment, the, 41
envisioning a better world, 9, 17, 59, 39–42, 60–62, 70–71, 73
epistemology, 82
eschatology, 32, 59
ethico-religious teleology, 9
ethics, 24, 49, 51
evil, 25, 33–34, 70
as egotism, deluded, 17, 41
monuments to egotism, examples of, 61
Exxon Mobil, 12, 39

F

Facebook, 39
faith
a Christian faith, 15
Calvin's maxim for faith, 10
conventional faith and mysticism, 45
in humans, 73
preeminence of faith, 5
fallacy, 23, 88
first-order moral principles, 51, 52
Flew, Antony ("Theology & Falsification"), 24, 43
discussion, 44–45, 55
caveats, 63, 72
Ford, Henry, 40
Fortuna, 72

Fourierism, 17
free will
   boundless, 12
   suffering, evil and, 25
   bounded, 51
freedom, 40, 51, 62, 70, 86
Freud, Sigmund
   and child development, 29, 35

G

Gandhi, Mohandas, 73
Gates, Bill, 41
Gates, John, 1–2
genocide, 61, 65
Gethsemane, 8
global economics, 13, 38, 39, 41
global market economy, 39
God
   a spirit, 16
   Deus Absconditus ("Hidden
      God"), 18
   as linguistic object, 20
   or *kosmos*, 23
   man's abandonment of, 24
   emotional, jealous, loving, 27
   Hebraic tribal God, 47–48
   auditory commands of, 11
   God's Extreme Makeover, 47
   wholly inscrutable, 48, 51, 56
   source of all value, 25, 27, 68
   as "ideal standard" of perfec-
      tion, reality, 68–69
   consciousness of, 72
God's will, 48, 51
goddesses, 65
Godhead, 69
gods
   and beasts, 36
   assume human form, 47
   fictitious, multiplicity of, 63
golden age, no, 41
Golden Calf, 18
Golden Rule, 52
Golgotha, 26
Google, 39

Gospels, 37
grace
   covenant of grace, 15
   Adamic fall from, 33
   natural grace and innocence, 60
   conditions of, 72
Graves, Robert, 3
Greek Myths, 3

H

Habitat for Humanity, 40
Halliburton, 12
Hare, R. M., 45
Hasidim, 45
Hauer, Christian E.
   influence as teacher and men-
      tor, 2
Hawking, Stephen, 55
Hegel, G. F. W., 56, 63
Hinduism, 46, 69
Hobbesian State of Nature, 15
holy shaman, 45
hubris, 32, 34, 41
human history, 17, 28, 34, 35
human nature
   unchanging, unlikely to change,
      29, 40
   prone to sin yet essentially
      good, 33
   limitations and vulnerabilities,
      47
   uniform and homogeneous the
      world over, 34
   seeking human betterment, 17
   human capacity for action, 40
   concern with human ethics and
      justice, 24
human inability
   versus corporate clout, 12
   to know God, 18
   to distinguish persons from
      their actions, 53
   to acquire supersensuous cog-
      nition, 56
   human limitations, 13, 47

human inability *(continued)*
    limits of imagination, understanding, 23
    Hutchinson, Anne, 14–15

I

ideas of reason, 56
imagination
    and contextual existence of gods, 74
    and moral thinking, 53
    and the goal of social science, 29
    child-like faith and salvation, 5
    communication and social improvement, 71
    limits and understanding, 23
immortality
    striving for, and hubris, 32
    and relative, 62
individuals, 40, 41, 53, 74
infanticide, 36
International Socialism, 17
Islam, 9, 16, 24, 45, 70
James, Henry, 14
James, William, 7
Jaspers, Karl, 25

J

Jesus
    life-mission, 4–5, 27, 28
    life as exemplary, 14
    unique development, 17
    central teaching, 26, 75
    emphasis on natality, 28
    preached
      action, 29
    concerned with "death-in-life," 33–36
    the temple metaphor, 37–39
    a new discovery in human consciousness, 47
    an evolution in divinity, 48

compassion, precept and practice, 54
as a standard for humans, 49
resurrection of the body, 59–62
isomorphism of religions, a single divine will, 62
achievement and immortality, 62
John Findley Green Lecture, 2
Johnson, Lyndon, 73
Jones, Jim, 12
Judeo-Christian heritage, 2, 14, 50, 70
judgment
    need for forbearance, 8
    what derails one's, 52, 53
    vindictive, 70
    enhanced, 73

K

Kant, Immanuel
    constraint on morality, 29, 29n1
    morality and freedom, 51
    conventional vs. critical morality, 51–52
    form of Moral Law, 54
    achievement in *Critique of Pure Reason*, 56, 63
    on modern science, 86
Kierkegaard, Søren, 1, 33
King, Martin Luther, Jr., 73
Kingdom of Thumôs, 27, 28
knowledge
    acquisition of, 25. *See also* Appendix II, 82–89
Koop, C. Everett, 73

L

labor movements, 17
law of double-negation, 44
laws of nature, 9
laws of physics, 51
Lincoln, Abraham, 34n2
Lucretius, 74

Luther, Martin, 18, 25

M

magic, 65, 66
Malcolm X (Malcolm Little), 73
Malraux, André, 61
marketing
    origins of, 14
    America's, 16, 37, 38
    unholy specter of, 18
    essentially manipulative, 62
    "School of the Americas," 70
maxims (four)
    for faith, 10
    practical, 54
    Biblical, 69
    Nietzsche, 69–70
Miller, Alice
    child abuse and violence, 29
    "soul-murder" of children,
        35–36
    and parent-child relationship,
        46–47
    and "resurrection of the body,"
        60–61
Miller, Perry, 3, 9
    Puritan scholarship, "The Mar-
        row of Puritan Divinity," 14
    profound religious experience,
        15
monotheism, 14, 16, 27, 66, 69
Monroe, Marilyn, 65
morality and resurrection, 5
    America's need for, 8
    and ethico-religious teleology, 9
    limitations of, 29
morality and religion
    proper relationship of, 50, 57
    beauty of, 52
    and human freedom, 51
    religion and legalism, 50
Mosaic Law, 47
Muhammad, 16, 69
mysticism, 2, 45, 91
    and poetry, mythology, 2

N

Nahum, the Book of, 47–48, 48n1
natality, 28
nature
    laws of, 9
    physical, limits of, 21, 22
    planet and natural world, 38
    Nature or God, 61
    physical nature, 85
Nature's Nation, 38
Nazi Germany, 34
New Age, 43, 64
Newman, Paul, 65
Newton's hypertrophic Physicist,
    27
Nietzsche, Friedrich, 24, 69, 70
No Name God, 16, 18, 24

O

Oliver Twist, 38
one true God, 56, 69
opinion-sharing and consensus,
    8, 10, 36, 53, 71. *See also*
    Arendt, Hannah
    concept of authority; Jesus and
    action

P

pantheism, 69
parent-child relationship, 46
Parmenides, 46
paternalism, 34
Peirce, Charles, 7, 89
Pentagon, 12
perfection
    an idle dream, 61
    existence as a, 64
    as mere attribute, 67
    as a standard of measurement,
        68
    belonging to God, 69
    Fourth Way (The Moral Argu-
        ment), 79

perfection *(continued)*
  Second Proof, 81
Phantom Zone, 66
phenomenology, 2, 48
philanthropy, 40
philosophy
  and mind, 24
  and logic, 31
  boundaries between . . . and, 46
  theory of knowledge, 82
Pitt, Brad, 65
Plato, 9, 27, 36, 64, 68
Pol Pot, 61
politics
  religion and, 15
  as primary institution, 32
  and profit-maximization, 38
  and stamp of shared mortality,
    57
  and the sublime, 72
  and logic, human nature, 82
polytheism, discussed, 16
  in antiquity, female-dominated,
    27, 47, 65
Posterior Analytics, 64
practical benefits
  four:
    1) illuminates whole of
    Christian thought, 4, 5; 2)
    relevant to contemporary
    America, 22; 3) nine argu-
    ments, their merit and
    import, 5, 18–24, appraisal,
    authenticity, 43–45, 50–51,
    53–57, rehabilitated moral
    argument, 64, 67–69; 4)
    clarifies relationship of disci-
    plinary science and religion,
    72, 73, 74
principle of sufficient reason,
    56n1–n3
*Principle of Sufficient Reason, On
  . . . the*, 63
profit-maximization, 38, 42
Protestant Reformation, the, 13

psychotherapy, 28

Q

Q'ur'an, 46

R

Ramayana, 3, 46
reasons, 8, 64, 70, 85, 89
Reformation, 9, 28, 36, 40
religion
  and atheism, 74
  and empirical knowledge, 24
  and meaning, 4, 13, 37, 63, 64,
    74
  organized religion, 32, 34, 35
  religious activism, 15
  defense of, 34
  sister religions, 16, 24, 48
  supernatural claims, 25
  without propositions, 45
Renaissance, 28, 36, 71
resurrection, 4, 5, 29, 59, 60, 62
  and Alice Miller, 60–61
  Christian theology, 5, 59
  Christian eschatology, 32
revelation, 45
rhetorical fallacies, 4, 23, 88
Ricoeur, Paul, 2, 33
Rockefeller, John D., 41
Romans, 13
Russell, Bertrand, 19, 31, 82, 85
Ruth, 27

S

salvation
  individual and collective, 5
  and self-examination, 10
  and the holy, 26
  unfolding of personality, 27
  and unpredictability, 36
  counterfeit, 51
  true salvation, 61
Scholem, Gershom, 46

Schopenhauer, Arthur, 24, 55
 considered view of human history, 34
 criticism of Descartes, 64
 on Kant's achievement, Hegel's failure, 56, 63
 sensation and intellection distinguished, 55
science, 5
 ontological assumption of science, 22
 kosmos . . .and science, 23
 limits of metaphysics, 24
 Argument from Design, 23, 80
 "new science," limits of, 28
 and capitalism, 36
 social science and human imagination, 29
 and primary institutions, 32
 developed sciences, structure of, 45, 86
 limits of empirical science, 73
 improved on sin? 32
 behavioral sciences and media, 32–33
Scorsese, Martin, 48
Scripture, 26, 32, 35
 scripture, 3, 5, 14, 69
secularization
 historic, 14
 Harry Ausmus, 24
 and culminating of consciousness, 28–29
 capitalism the chief vehicle of, 38–39
 and Christian eschatology, 59
self-delusion, 34, 52
Shakers, 45
sin, 4, 33, 36, 59
Sita, 27
Socrates, 8, 89
"Son of Man," 28
Sophocles, 31
"soul-murder," 35

Space Age Mythology, The (seminar), 2
Spears, Britney, 65
Stace, Walter, 46
Star Wars, 7
Stebbing, Paul, 13, 13n2
Stoddard, Solomon, 14
sublime, 46, 57, 65, 72
Stalin, Joseph, 61
Sufis, 45

T

Tao Te Ching, 3
Taoism, 69
tautologous, 19
tautology, 20, 85, 87
Taylor, Liz, 65
Taylor, Richard, 55
technological change, 8
Ten Commandments, 50
Teresa of Avila, 46
The Cambridge Platform of 1648, 3, 9
The Critique of Pure Reason 56
"The Death of Ivan Ilyich," 32
The Last Temptation of Christ, 48
The Natural Child Project, 60
The White Goddess, 27
theology
 practical benefits of, 5, 69
 purpose of, 15
 meaning of death for, 32
 psychotherapy and sin, 33
 speculative theology, impossibility of, 56
 an empirical matter, 73
thumôs, thumoeides, 27
Tillich, Paul, 1, 25
Tolstoy, Leo, 32
transcendence, 31
truths of mathematics, 68, 85

U

unity of religions, synonymy of scriptures, 69
utilitarianism, 34

V

value
   source of all, 25, 27, 35
   and human aspiration, 41
   and profit-maximization, 42
Vietnam, 2
Volsung Saga, 3

W

Walmart, 39

Weber, Max, 29
Wilde, Oscar, 32
William Arthur Young (Bill Young), 3, 24
Williams, Roger, 14, 15
Wisdom, John, 44
Wittgenstein, Ludwig, 13n1
Wordsworth, William, 4, 4n2, 29, 35

Y

Yahveh, 47, 65, 66, 69

Z

Zevi, Sabbatai, 12
Zohar the Book of Splendor, 46

www.ingramcontent.com/pod-product-compliance
Lightning Source LLC
Chambersburg PA
CBHW070508090426
42735CB00012B/2694